What Makes the Gospel So Irreplaceable

What Makes the Gospel So Irreplaceable

Exploring the Three Unique Qualities of the Gospel

Hendry Ongkowidjojo

WIPF & STOCK · Eugene, Oregon

WHAT MAKES THE GOSPEL SO IRREPLACEABLE
Exploring the Three Unique Qualities of the Gospel

Wipf & Stock
An Imprint of Wipf and Stock Publishers
199 W. 8th Ave., Suite 3
Eugene, OR 97401

www.wipfandstock.com

PAPERBACK ISBN: 978-1-4982-8928-3
HARDCOVER ISBN: 978-1-4982-8930-6
EBOOK ISBN: 978-1-4982-8929-0

Manufactured in the U.S.A.

To Elisabeth Liauw

Contents

Preface

It is not that I don't believe in Jesus," she says, "but I struggle with believing that there's only one path to God. I wonder about things like, if God is all-forgiving, then why won't you go to heaven if you don't believe in Christ? And how could a loving God require Jesus to suffer and die on a cross?[1]

IN THEIR BOOK *MOVE*, authors Greg Hawkins and Cally Parkinson tell a story about Marcia, whose husband, Rick, goes to church after recently losing his job that he had held for twenty-four years. The couple faithfully attends worship meetings since from then on. They "think highly of their pastor and often take advantage of different classes the church offers on faith-related questions and topics."[2] All this shows that the couple is serious about their faith. However, even after two years of being an active explorer, Marcia "is not yet ready to fully accept all that Christ taught." What we quoted above is the reason for her struggle.

Few people today are bothered by Christians' claim that we are saved in Jesus Christ. But we won't get away that easily with the claim that Jesus is the *only* way of salvation. In this global and pluralistic era there is a huge pressure to admit that there are many hopes for salvation. Today, Christians who make such a claim will be deemed, at best, as naïve and, at worst, as arrogant and uncivilized.

---

1. Hawkins and Parkinson, *Move*.
2. Ibid., 31

This kind of judgment occurs because, as John Piper has said, this postmodern era often "confuses uncertainty with humility." According to him, "'Arrogance' is the condemnation of choice in the political and religious arena for anyone who breaks the rules of relativism." Moreover, "One mark of that culture is the hijacking of the word *arrogance* to refer to *conviction,* and the word *humility* to refer to *uncertainty.*"[3]

Postmodernism aside, I also see that many people dislike our claim because they only know *what* Christians believe but not *why* they believe it. Like Marcia above, many people know only the *conclusion* but not the *reason;* only the *statement* but not the *explanation.* That is why they are furious, or at least struggle, when we insist that Christ is the only way of salvation. It is important for us to realize how big the statement "Jesus is the *only* way of salvation" is. If I said, "You are about to read the most important book in your entire life, because this book is second to none," I believe I would be more likely to get antipathy than a nod of agreement from you. You would naturally think, "Who do you think you are?" Therefore, it is natural if many struggle to accept the exclusivity of Christ without enough understanding.

For the remedy, Hawkins and Parkinson suggest a balance of two things. First of all, "It is important to give people the space to make their own decisions—a process that may take a different amount of time for each individual."[4] However, this alone is not enough because "if people wait too long, they tend to grow apathetic and are less likely to ever accept Christ." Therefore, for the balancing act, "at the same time we give them opportunities to explore, *we must also give them reasons to believe*" (emphasis added).

And that is what this book will try to accomplish: give reasons to believe. As Peter said, "But in your hearts honor Christ the Lord as holy, always being prepared to make a defense to anyone who asks you for a reason for the hope that is in you; yet do it with gentleness and respect" (1 Pet 3:15). This book is not about blaming or dishonoring other faiths, nor about merely propagating or

3. Piper, *Brothers,* 159–66.
4. Hawkins and Parkinson, *Move,* 43.

pumping our faith, but about understanding, enjoying, and be convinced of the hope that is embedded in our faith, so that we know that "to tell this gospel is not arrogant but loving."[5]

In Romans 1:16–17 we will explore three unique qualities of the gospel: it is powerful, righteous, and by faith alone. However, among these three we will spend most of our time comprehending how the gospel displays God's righteousness as clearly as it displays God's love. It is because today's discussion of salvation touches the element of righteousness only rarely. People of the twenty-first century talk about salvation as if nothing else mattered except God's love or mercy. Raising the subject of God's justice and his wrath over sins is deemed rude, intolerant, or merciless.

In my opinion, this exaltation of God's mercy out of proportion is one main reason why many Christians are ashamed of the gospel and find it hard to have a much-needed assurance. Because of this, so many Christians bear a question similar to Marcia's above. If God is all-forgiving, how could he choose only one way of salvation? If God is merciful, surely he will try to save as many human as possible. A loving God could not be stingy, could he?

The remedy is again found in balancing God's love and God's righteousness. Of course we are not supposed to deny God's love. But we must hold it hand in hand with his righteousness. And this truth comes from the Bible itself, especially if we carefully follow Paul's arguments. Thus, *by exploring Romans 1:16–17, this book will show why righteousness matters: once we put God's righteousness into the "terms and conditions" of how to be saved, there is simply no other way of salvation but through faith in Jesus Christ alone.*

I would like to thank my wife, Shirley Liz, and my son, Lincoln, for the many ways of support they have provided me. Rev. Dr. Stephen Tong has encouraged me to write my first book, and for that I am truly grateful. Thanks also to Tirza, who has spent her time editing the content of this book. I would also like to mention the coworkers who have faithfully shared the privilege of proclaiming the gospel with me from one hospital to another. And finally, this book is dedicated to Elisabeth Liauw, who was my

5. Piper, *Brothers*, 164.

youth mentor and without whom I would not have become who I am today.

To God be the glory.

I

I Am Not Ashamed of
the Gospel, Am I?

WHAT DID PAUL AND Alexander the Great have in common?
History records show they had a similar hobby: they loved trav-
elling and could not stay long in one place. Alexander the Great
travelled 19,900 miles in his life, while Paul in his missionary activity scored 15,500 miles. Not a bad comparison by any means.[1]

Even the purpose of their journey was quite similar: to con-
quer as many nations as possible. The difference was that while
Alexander took the nations for himself, Paul was eager to present
them to Christ. He travelled that far to share the gospel for the
glory of Jesus Christ.

In Acts and in Paul's letters we read how he moved tirelessly
from one place to another, never satisfied with what he had achieved,
always setting his eyes for more. For Paul, getting the job done in one
place meant only one thing: going forth to another place. In Romans
15:23 Paul says, "But now, since I no longer have any room for work
in these regions, and since I have longed for many years to come to
you, I hope to see you in passing as I go to Spain, and to be helped
on my journey there by you, once I have enjoyed your company for

---

1. Schnabel, *Early Christian Mission*, 1288. Schnabel also provides more
detail information: "A conservative estimate indicates that Paul traveled about
25,000 km (ca. 15,500 mi.) between his conversion in AD 31/32 and his execution in AD 67, including 14,000 km (ca. 8,700 mi.) on foot, a distance that
required 660 days of overland travel" (p. 1478).

a while." There was no more room for his work there? For Paul, it could only have meant another region was waiting for him.

We read of a similar attitude in Acts. According to the traditions, Paul is known to have made three far-reaching missionary journeys during his life, and the time gap between the second and the third journey provides us with an interesting discovery. Where in Acts can we find the end of the second missionary journey? The answer is in verse 18:22. And where can we find the beginning of the third one? You can read about it in 18:23! It looks like Paul was the kind of man who'd stay in bed only if it's his death bed.

How different is today's situation! Not only are we not eager to share the gospel, but the gospel often looks like a torment to many believers. Many of us will find it hard to count how many sermons about evangelism we have heard since we became Christians. But only few of us will find any difficulty in counting how many times we actually *tell* the gospel to the people around us. For most of us, the number amounts to scarcely more than the fingers on our hand.

It seems like no matter how hard some pastors have pushed, their congregations hardly move even a bit. To encourage his congregation to share the gospel, one pastor I know personally put a vase of white roses near the pulpit. He then challenged his congregation that he would add one rose for every person who was won for Christ. And the result? After one year not a single rose was added. When the topic is sharing the gospel, it is easier to discourage rather than to encourage even adamant pastors.

Is this not a huge irony? Etymologically speaking, the gospel means "good news." The gospel is even *the* good news. If this is so, then how has this *good* news become such a *bad* news—not only for the outsider, but even for believers themselves? It looks like the gospel is an unbearable burden for the church, both for the pastor and the people.

What made Paul so different? Why didn't he ever think of retiring from sharing the gospel, while we never think of starting? On the one hand, we know Paul had been called for sharing the gospel, especially to the Gentiles (see Rom 1:3). This awareness of divine calling was ever-replenished fuel until the end of his life. It kept reminding him of his being "under obligation both to Greeks and to barbarians, both to the wise and to the foolish," and made him "eager to preach the gospel to you also who are in Rome" (Rom 1:14, 15).

Thus Paul was different from us because he had a distinct calling. Therefore, it is understandable if we have no such zeal for the gospel, because our calling is different to his . . . right? Wrong! While Paul's calling was indeed different from us, it wasn't the one and only reason for his great zeal for the gospel. Similarly, while most of us are not called to be a missionary like him, our small affection for the gospel has another cause.

In Romans 1:15–16 we read: "I am eager to preach the gospel to you also who are in Rome. *For* I am not ashamed of the gospel . . ." (emphasis added). In his fine commentary on Romans, Douglas Moo says, "Paul's *pride* in the gospel (v. 16a) is the reason why he is so eager to preach the gospel in Rome (v. 15)" (emphasis added).[2] Hence we can detect two reasons for Paul's eagerness to preach the gospel in Rome: not only because he was called, but also because he was not ashamed of the gospel. Paul was proud of the gospel, therefore he could not stop talking about it wherever he went.

And the opposite is exactly what we experience. We may agree that each and every Christian has his or her own distinct calling. Not all of us are called to be like D. L. Moody, who couldn't sleep at night if he had not shared the gospel to at least one person earlier that day. But the other reason we are not too eager to share the gospel is because talking about it to strangers make us feel uneasy—we are ashamed of it.

I remember when I was still in the high school I attended a revival. After the revival was over, my friends and I went to a mall to have a late dinner. The mall was right next to the revival meeting, so we went there directly after the meeting. And I tried to hide my Bible so that the crowd in the mall could not see me bringing it. Can you imagine it? I tried to hide the Bible right after I attended

2. Moo, *Romans*, 63.

a revival! I was afraid of what people might think of me bringing the Bible inside the mall. I was so ashamed of the Bible, and of the gospel inside.

But how can we handle this feeling of shame? I believe no true Christian enjoys being ashamed of the gospel. We long to love the gospel, to share it bravely, even to defend it in front of many people; do we not? But our feeling betrays us: instead of finding courage, we become afraid and back off. We act contrary to Paul; we are ashamed of the gospel through which God has mightily saved us. How can we handle this?

It is important to make a distinction between our feeling and the reason behind it. Shame is certainly connected with our feeling. We *feel* ashamed, right? However, the *feeling* of shame and its *cause* are two different matters. While shame is related to our feeling, its cause is related to our *understanding*.

The feeling of shame itself does not have to be equal to making a mistake. A feeling of shame is proper if it is grounded upon a proper understanding. We should, for example, be ashamed of sinning because feeling fine with our sin shows a defect in understanding. But feeling shame about the gospel is an improper thing, caused by improper understanding.

Therefore, instead of dealing directly with our feeling, it would be more effective to take one step further and see the reason behind it. *Why* are we ashamed of the gospel instead of proud of it? On the contrary, *what made* Paul so eager about the gospel? What was *the reason* behind it?

We should be grateful, for in Romans 1:16–17 we find not only Paul's confidence of the gospel but also the reason behind it. It will do us good to read carefully what Paul says in these key verses:

> For I am not ashamed of the gospel, for it is the power of God for salvation to everyone who believes, to the Jew first and also to the Greek. For in it the righteousness of God is revealed from faith for faith, as it is written, "The righteous shall live by faith."

We need to see the flow of argument within these verses. Paul built his argument brick by brick. Each sentence is built upon the last one and supports the next one.[3] Why was Paul not ashamed of the gospel? It is because Paul knew that the gospel is the power of God for salvation. And what makes the gospel the power of God for salvation? Because the gospel reveals the righteousness of God by faith alone. Or in another words, because Paul saw that the gospel reveals the righteousness of God by faith alone, therefore he understood that the gospel is so powerful. And because he knew that the gospel is so powerful for all who believe, he had no reason to be ashamed of it. Paul's understanding of the gospel was the ground for how he felt about it.

This book will unveil Paul's rich understanding of the gospel in this passage, to find the essence of Paul's conviction. We would like to know why for Paul the gospel is so irreplaceable. In the next chapters we will find three things of utmost importance in Romans 1:16–17 which make the gospel so different from any other ways of salvation, which in turn are the reasons why Paul was not ashamed of it: (1) the gospel is the power of God (chapter 2); (2) the gospel has revealed the righteousness of God (chapters 3–9); (3) the salvation that comes from the gospel is by faith alone (chapters 10–11). The second point will be the most discussed, because it is the ground for the first and the third one.

Understanding these three reasons will greatly help us to see what makes the gospel is so irreplaceable. And let us hope that, by the grace of God, recognizing this unique quality of the gospel will boost our pride in this most precious thing in our life: the gospel itself. Let the journey begin!

---

3. According to Moo, "These theologically dense verses are made up of four subordinate clauses, each supporting or illuminating the one before it" (ibid., 63).

II

The Gospel as God's Power

LET START WITH AN analogy from our daily life. Let's say a member of my congregation has recently gambled and lost a huge amount of money. This loss is such a huge one that all his wealth is drained and his business ruined. As a servant of God, what should I do? How could I help this poor fellow?

I have at least three choices. (1) I can come to him, rebuke him, and let him see what a foolish mistake he has made. I may confront him harshly. As a Christian, how could he not know better than falling into such greed? (2) I can come to him with the deepest sympathy and words of encouragement. After helping him see his sin and its consequences, I can sit beside him, feel deeply for his condition, and pray that God will pour his patience and mercy on him. Finally, (3) I can give him advice. I can help him make up his mind and start brand new all over again.

Which approach is the best one? All of them are good and necessary, are they not? Sinners must be rebuked because there is no hope for an unrepentant sinner. However, rebuke alone is inadequate. After helping him realize his own mistake, he still needs a word of encouragement to help him endure the heavy burdens caused by his sin. Finally, it will be extremely helpful if we can give workable advice to help him rebuild his life.

However—and this is important—although all of these approaches are extremely helpful, all of them are only *words*. Whether I rebuke, encourage, or advise him, what I give is words and nothing else. I may take actions like getting into my car, driving to his house, sitting next to him, and even praying earnestly for him. Still what I have done first and foremost is the speech-act.

No matter how good and helpful my words are, no matter how thankful he is for them, we know from experience that for someone in his situation they are not much of a help. They do not have much power left.

But what if, after I am done with rebuking, encouraging, and giving him advise, I say to him, "How much is your debt? How much do you need to rebuild your life brand new? Take all this money. It will be enough to cover all that you need. Don't bother about paying it back. Take this to pay all your debts and rebuild your business. I love you and want to see you rise out of your fallen state. May God bless you!"

Did I hear you say "Wow!"? This fourth approach is totally different, is it not? In a different league by all measure. And what makes this approach so different from the previous ones? Because this time I do not only speak but also act, and act decisively.

By offering him the money to pay for all his losses, I do not only give him words. My last action contains power. I do not only show him the way he should take to rebuild his life, but I *actually* rebuild his life. The decisive factor does not lie in his response, but in my action. He knows he is not only listening to "the way of salvation"; he knows he is being saved!

By analogy, this is what God has done for us in the gospel: he has paid for all of our debts. Of course I do not mean that God lends us spiritual treasure so that we may pay our spiritual debt. The story above is simply an illustration, and it is not wise to read too much into it. But hopefully this simple illustration helps us to see what Paul means when he declared that the gospel "is the power of God for salvation to everyone who believes" (Rom 1:18). Not only does God give us instructions for salvation, and not only does he guide us to fulfill those instructions, but he actually and in reality *saves* us; he provides everything it takes for our salvation.

On the one hand, the gospel surely cannot be separated from word. We *listen* to the gospel and *share* the gospel. The gospel rebukes sins, encourages the hopeless in this world, and shows us a true way of salvation. But on the other hand, the gospel is not just that. In the gospel God does not only speak; he acts decisively. Without making us into passive pre-programmed robots, God already provides everything needed for our salvation. The gospel is indeed the power of God for our salvation.

Moo shows that the meaning of the word "power" must be understood according to its Old Testament background. Moo refers to "the OT teaching about a personal God who uniquely possesses power and who manifests that power in delivering (Exod 9:16; Ps 77:14–15) and judging (Jer 16:21) his people."[1] Understanding this Old Testament background will help us greatly in our effort of understanding what Paul means by "power."

In its story of the Exodus, the Old Testament consistently and continually speaks of the salvation of Israel from Egypt as the act of God *alone*. Thus, instead of saying, "*We both* know how *our* beloved Israel has been ruthlessly enslaved by their conqueror. Therefore, let *us* work together to bring them back from their exile," God consistently said,

> *I* have surely seen the affliction of my people who are in Egypt and have heard their cry because of their taskmasters. *I* know their sufferings, and *I* have come down to deliver them out of the hand of the Egyptians and to bring them up out of that land to a good and broad land . . . And now, behold, the cry of the people of Israel has come to *me*, and *I* have also seen the oppression with which the Egyptians oppress them. Come, *I* will send you to Pharaoh that you may bring *my* people, the children of Israel, out of Egypt." (Exod 3:7–10, emphasis added)

Thus, while Moses and Aaron were clearly called to deliver Israel from Egypt, the Exodus was the act of God *alone*. He was the one who came down, the one who delivered, the one who led Israel to the Promise Land. The great Old Testament Exodus is the power of *God* for Israel's salvation. Therefore, when Israel later celebrated the Passover, they were not remembering what the famous

1. Ibid., 66.

trio God, Moses and Aaron, had done for them. The Passover is to God's praise *alone*.

Reading the entire story of Exodus will also show that the deliverance of Israel is a sure thing: there is not even the slightest possibility that Israel will end remaining slaves of the Egyptians. The Exodus happened simply because there was no possibility it did not happen; *God* made sure it happened!

And the reason is not that Egypt was so weak at that time, nor that Israel could have mastered their weaponry and used it to strike back; it was because of God, and God *alone*. That Israel in the end actually left Egypt was *only* because God manifested his mighty power upon Egypt. It was God who made their fiend totally helpless. The Exodus, without denying humans' part in it, was determined *decisively* by God's hand alone.

With this Old Testament background in mind, when Paul stated that the gospel is the power of God for salvation to everyone who believes, he saw the same decisive act of God as the deliverance of Israel out of Egypt. Although Paul had been called to share the gospel among the Gentiles, as Moses had been called to go to Egypt, not even for a moment did he forget that "we have this treasure in jars of clay, to show that the surpassing power belongs to God and not to us" (2 Cor 4:7). God *alone,* through the redemptive act of Jesus Christ, has saved those who believe in the gospel.

Therefore when we celebrate the Passover or partake of Holy Communion, we do not celebrate our partnership in the gospel. Similar to Israel celebrating the Passover, in the Holy Communion we are celebrating what God *alone* has done to save us.

Understanding that the gospel is God's power for salvation is very important for understanding why the gospel is different from any other good news or ways of salvation. In some religions, humankind can be saved because one among them has found the way of salvation without help from above and then shared his good news to as many people as possible.[2] In others, their God has

---

2. Some Buddhists that I have met are quite sure that God plays no role in Buddhism. But see Yandell and Netland, *Buddhism*, 12.

revealed the path of salvation; he has given a set of laws that must be followed in order for one can be saved.

But the Christian's gospel is different. In the gospel we are saved by God's power *alone*. In the gospel God does not just give us instructions for salvation, but he actually and decisively *saves* us. The gospel is not a list from God containing dos and don'ts for those who want to be saved. Through the gospel God actually and actively saves us.

Paul saw clearly that the gospel could never fail. He knew this was not because he was so strong, but because "I know whom I have believed, and I am convinced that he is able to guard until that Day what has been entrusted to me" (2 Tim 1:12). That is why Paul was able to declare the gospel as the power of God. That is why he found no reason whatsoever to be ashamed of the gospel.

We must wait until a couple of chapters later to see what exactly God has done in the gospel that makes it so powerful. But for now we need to realize that the gospel's power is the one that makes it so unique. For others, at the end of the day, what oneself has done is decisive. For the gospel, the most decisive factor is what God has done. This is the one very important thing that separates the gospel from all other ways of salvation. Not only Paul, but every believer who understands that the gospel is not only word but power, may boast with him. Indeed, how could you be ashamed of such failure-proof good news as the gospel?

III

Love, Emotion, Salvation

WHAT IS THE BEST-KNOWN verse in the Bible? If we could do a survey we might come up with two possible answers: (1) "I do not know and/or I do not care," or (2) "For God so loved the world, that he gave his only Son, that whoever believes in him should not perish but have eternal life." John 3:16 is widely regarded as the most important and beautiful passage in the Bible. It is also the most-quoted one. In this verse we can find both the handiest and the deepest statement about the love of God. And what could be more beautiful and meaningful than a God who is full of love?

If we did a similar survey about the best-known teaching of Jesus, the winner would most probably not be "go therefore and make disciples of all nations" (Matt 28:18) or "the kingdom of heaven is at hand" (Matt 10:7), but "if anyone slaps you on the right cheek, turn to him the other also . . . love your enemies" (Matt 5:39, 44). Even for those who do not believe in Jesus as Lord, this teaching is still regarded as the Golden Rule, the one that put Jesus once and for all among the maha gurus in the history of humankind.

All these show the central place of love in Christianity. Although history records that Christians often fail to get an excellent score in the love examination, even today "love" seems inseparable from the church. Buddhism may be closely related with "peace,"[1]

---

1. According to Yandell and Netland, "The Buddha offers many a vision of inner peace and tranquility in an age marked by high stress, rampart materialism, and consumerism" (ibid., ix).

and Moslem with "zeal," but "love" seems closer to Christianity. Therefore it might be difficult to digest if I propose that, at least recently, the term "love" is the very thing that has become a huge stumbling block for Christianity; for many Christians today, it is exactly God's love that makes the gospel *replaceable*. Will you raise your eyebrows if I say that many Christians today are ashamed of the gospel simply because they *do* believe in God's love? Is it too weird to be true?

Let us once again make a survey. Let us ask those who were Christian but are not anymore, "Why are you no longer a Christian?" Why did you leave the church?" I do not think you will be too surprised if I say that one major answer is *disappointment*. Most of us who have been a Christian for long enough may personally know people who said goodbye to God because of this very reason. Some of us may even know pastors or missionaries who left their congregation and their field because they were disappointed.

What is critical for our topic is that while some of them were disappointed by other Christians, by their congregation, or by their pastor, some see *God* as the one who disappointed them. And if our survey digs deep enough, we will see that one character trait of God that made them bitter is his *love*: they feel God's love is not up to their expectations and is less than what they heard, read, or hope for. They have thrown away their faith because, according to their *understanding*, God loves them less than he promised he would.

In this fallen world, a wrong understanding of God's love means danger! An improper understanding of God's love has caused so many Christians to leave the church. And the same mistake makes so many of us uneasy to declare, "And there is salvation in *no one else*, for there is *no other name* under heaven given among men by which we must be saved" (Acts 4:12, emphasis added). An improper understanding of God's love has caused so many Christians to be ashamed of the gospel.

We will spend a bit more time discussing the phenomenon of this people leaving church because it may help us clarify our issue. Then we will see how this phenomenon is so similar to our main topic. Hopefully we will start to see that as great as God's love is, an improper understanding of it could be disastrous.

Many people have left the church because they heard and believed so many promises about God's love that have no foundation whatsoever in the Bible. Today we hear slogans like "God loves you and that is why he will not let you suffer. Trust him with all your heart for he will not let you poor or leave you with your sickness. He will bless you abundantly and heal you completely." Someone who regularly and continually listen to such a message will quickly relate God's love with health, success, and prosperity. And when they are ill, unsuccessful, or not rich, they will be easily tempted to think that something must be wrong.

In the beginning they may see themselves as the guilty ones. Some preachers will quickly tell them that they should trust God more. Or they will be informed that they need to remember and confess their sins with as much detail as possible. However, the problem will escalate if, after trying so hard to believe in God and recollecting every minute detail of their sins, those who are sick remain sick, those who are in trouble remain in trouble, and those who are poor remain poor. It's only a matter of time until they start to point their finger at God, the "liar."

What is the root of the problem? It is *not* God's love itself but our improper understanding of it. There is no promise whatsoever in the Bible that if we are Christians and if our faith is strong enough then we will become free of trouble. This kind of understanding of God's love does not go back to Bible. We exalt God's love improperly, and that makes us so vulnerable.

God promises us strength and guidance, but as long as we live in this fallen world the problem of evil is as real for believers as for unbelievers. This is a fact no one can deny: until Christ comes for the second time, the rate of dying people among Christians and non-Christians will be exactly the same; both will be a perfect 100 percent. All human being simply have to die, whether they are inside or outside of Christ.

In relation to our topic, the very same mistake often makes Christians ashamed of the gospel. In a sense, many Christians dare not affirm Christ as the only salvation *not* because they doubt the love of God in him, but because they are afraid of limiting God's love. For them, as I have written in the preface, "If God is love, how could he choose only one way of salvation? If God is merciful, surely he will try to save as many human as possible, through as many ways as possible. A loving God could not be stingy, could he?"

Can anyone with this concept in his or her mind firmly believe that there is no salvation outside Christ? Or even if he or she can't help but believe that real redemption is only in Christ, will he or she not then try to extend the definition of those who are saved in Christ as wide as possible? An inaccurate understanding of God's love can cause some Christians to leave their faith out of disappointment, and make others ashamed of the gospel.

Moreover, what makes the water murkier is that many of us understand love as equal with our feelings. Romantic love is all around today. And romantic love is almost always equated with living *happily* ever after.

In relation to our understanding of salvation, it can be said that if a concept of salvation makes me feel good then I will accept it; if it makes me feel bad then I will reject it. If an idea of salvation touches me to the point of tears then it must be right, but if it agitates me or makes me feel uneasy then it must be wrong. This improper emphasis of love and feeling is the *main* cause of many contemporary misunderstandings of the gospel.

Many object to Christ being the only way of salvation not because they have proven it to be *wrong*, but because they *feel* uneasy declaring it. Consider accusations you may have heard: "How could you say that salvation is only in Christ? Isn't that selfish and intolerant? What about our ancestors? Dare you say that they will not be saved because they did not believe in Christ, of whom they never heard?"

Later we will address especially this last question, but for now please take note that the purpose of accusations such as "how dare you . . . ?" or "how could you . . . ?" or "what kind of man are you . . . ?" is to make us *feel* guilty and bad. This kind of argument does not attack our minds as strong as it attacks our feelings. Salvation is no longer a matter of right or wrong, but more a matter of good or bad, generous or stingy, kindness or rude, etc.

We have to admit that sometimes we are too insensitive to other people's feelings when sharing the gospel. Furthermore, because for more than a thousand years Christianity has been identified with the West, and therefore with its imperialism, the stigma of colonialism has become the burden of Christianity today. My country was itself under the oppression of Holland, a Protestant country, for more than two hundred years. Declaring that Christ is the sole savior not only for the West but also for the East makes Christianity look like a new kind of invasion.

I do believe that sometimes we need to apologize for the many mistakes committed by us or by our fellow Christians. Paul's accusation at his fellow Jews is still very relevant for Christians today: "For, as it is written, 'The name of God is blasphemed among the Gentiles because of you'" (Rom 2:24). But even after saying all these, there is still no good reason to compromise the message of the gospel. It is very problematic to be ashamed of the gospel because it contains the possibility of making us look intolerant, cruel, or stingy. It is out of place, and even dangerous, to change our message of salvation just because we do not want to make people angry. And the very reason is because, as Richard Mouw has reminded all of us, "what we believe as Christians has to do with matters of eternal significance."[2]

We need to remember why we share the gospel. We do not share the gospel simply because this is our hobby or a relaxing experience, but because we want to bring others into the salvation that we already enjoy in Christ. And we are eager to bring them into salvation because we know what the only other option is. Salvation is needed because of sin, and people are to be saved from sin because the alternative is horrifying. Salvation is so crucial because sin and its consequences are so crucial. And when making any decision whose nature is so crucial, our feelings and preferences should not be allowed to be the sole and decisive factor.

As a comparison, if some people have cancer, then they have cancer whether they like it or not; how they feel may determine

2. Mouw, *Uncommon Decency*, 68.

how they will face their condition, but the condition of having cancer is simply a matter of fact. Furthermore, some of them may hate many Western things, but if they must have chemo treatment, they have no choice but to go to a Westernize hospital, whether they like or not. If they let their feelings take control they will suffer, or worse, they will die, as simple as that.

Finally—and this is extremely important—sin is not only a matter of fact, but also a matter of *judgment*. It is not possible to read the Bible and not find the vocabulary of the law court used to describe sin and anything that is related to it. In connection to sin and salvation, the Bible talks about a judge, throne, judgment, and punishment. All these words are taken from the realm of court and justice. And if salvation is a matter of justice, then unbridled love or uncontrolled feeling will bring more harm than help. For justice to work properly, love and feeling must be put in their proper place.

Imagine you become a judge, and in front of you is presented someone who has been convicted of murdering a whole family in a failed attempt at robbery. The lawyer tells you this is the man's first crime; he has no criminal record whatsoever. Besides, he has two dearly beloved children. The sole reason for his action is because he needed money for his children. Add to this the facts that his wife passed away, they have no relatives, and he is the only family his children have.

As the court proceeds, you clearly see that this accused murderer is actually a beloved and gentle father. You notice also that his children love him so much and they are so close with one another. You can even read their faces about how worried they are because they might no longer have a chance to see their father as a free man. Indeed, delivering this beloved father to jail means taking away the only person in the world who cares for them and loves them with his whole heart.

Now, it is time to make a decision. What are you going to decide? Guilty or not guilty? I do not think we will need to take a survey this time. You will judge this man as guilty, will you not? But why do you make such a decision? Is it because you are evil, rude, or heartless? Of course not! You will agree that all these terms are simply irrelevant here. You make such a decision because this man is *in fact* guilty and, according to *justice*, he must be punished.

We do not enjoy thinking of his future and are perplexed about what will happen to his children, but this uneasiness does not give us the right to decide differently. Whether he likes it or not, whatever his children will feel, and no matter whether you are able to sleep that night or not as you remember your decision, this man is guilty and the proper punishment must be given.

To go even further: A president may give this man presidential pardon, but even a president must not do so carelessly; he or she must follow the rule in doing so and must be able to give an account. That's why although all candidates for presidential election love to have a kind and merciful image, no one promises to release as many prisoners as possible once elected. No one will win with a campaign like this, for sure.

But why? Is it because citizens today prefer violence over love? Are they heartless? Are they not merciful enough, so they never think of how poor criminals cannot celebrate Thanksgiving in their homes with their families? Again and again we find that this kind of question is simply irrelevant.

All these examples warn us that, as we are talking about fact and judgment, we must be extremely careful in using the vocabulary of love, mercy, generosity, etc. Furthermore, we have seen enough that our preferences and our feelings must be strictly controlled once we enter into the realm of fact and justice.

Now, this is as true in this worldly law court as in the divine council. Exalting love improperly in the matter of sin and salvation will make evil more evil, and victims more victimized. That is why, even though God has the right to forgive sin, he will not (or dare we say cannot?) simply forgive and forget sin. Showing love carelessly will make the lover insulted and the love itself cheap.

God will do nothing that disregards himself. Everything he does will glorify himself. That is why in loving us God will not sacrifice his righteousness, because doing that would make him blameworthy. God's glory is in faithfully keeping his righteousness. As Calvin said, "He receives the full and complete praise which is His due only as He alone obtains the name and honor of being just."[3]

Any discussion of salvation should not forget that sin and salvation are matters of justice. I believe no one will deny that our God is *the* Great Judge. And a judge who is unjust or unrighteous is simply *not* great. We can wholeheartedly agree with Bonhoeffer that our salvation is free, but not cheap. And the very reason why our salvation is not cheap, although it is totally free, is this: when God saves us, he manifests both his love . . . and his righteousness.

3. Quoted in Schreiner, *Romans*, 199.

IV

The Gospel as God's Righteousness

ONCE I MET A Muslim whose belief surprised me. In the middle of our conversation I asked him, "According to your belief, how can human beings be saved and get to heaven?" His answer was quite different from what I used to get from other Muslims. In my previous experiences, many of them believe that three factors will determine their everlasting destiny: what they do in their lives, their legacies, and the prayers their sons and daughters offer on behalf of them after they pass away. But this one told me, "We Muslims, are saved merely by *rahmat Allah*," which means exactly "God's mercy."

Now, this answer is indeed interesting, and the more we talked the more I saw that his conviction is quite similar to mine. He did not say that good deeds are not important, but he was convinced that at the end of the day the most *decisive* factor is *rahmat Allah*. As in our previous discussion, while we do not deny human involvement, our salvation is definitely and ultimately in the hands of our God. On the other hand, while they do not deny that their God is full of mercy, other Muslims I have met have still referred to the requirements they have to fulfill to be saved according to their Qur'an. But this one was different.

As a response to his answer, I talked about God's righteousness. Like Christianity, Islam too believes in a God who is righteous, who knows of justice, and who will never do anything unjust. Actually, it is hard to imagine there is any religion that believes in God but does not believe that God is a righteous God.

Therefore, knowing that this Muslim believed in *rahmat Allah* for his salvation, I asked him a further question: "But how could the righteous God give his mercy instead of pour his wrath on *sinners*? Do we not believe that God must be the Righteous Judge? And if God insists on merely saving us despite of our sins and transgression, then how could he still be the righteous one?" I pushed a little bit more: "And how could God, after doing this, be able to answer Satan's accusation that he may be full with love but surely lacks justice for accepting sinners instead of punishing them properly? What do you think about this?"

His answer is still fresh in my mind: "In our faith, this is *ga'ib*," which means a mystery no one can fathom. As a response, I told him straightly but gently, "In our faith, Jesus Christ is *rahmat Allah*. In him God shows his ultimate love in saving us though we are nothing but sinners. *But* he does this without sacrificing even a bit of his justice. Therefore, in the Judgment Day, even Satan will have to admit that God is not only full of love and mercy, but also not lacking justice and righteousness." He did not make a decision to accept Christ at that moment, but it was clear that he was quite surprised by this fact of the gospel.

From this story we may see that salvation is more complex than what people may think today. Churchgoers are quick to say "Amen" when they hear their pastor declare, "God accepts sinners, does he not?" But what if he shouts, "A true judge releases those who are clearly guilty, does he not?" I do believe the response for the second statement will not be as enthusiastic as the first one, although both statements are the same in essence.

Sin makes things complicated and, accordingly, salvation from sin is not a simple matter. Therefore, it is naïve to talk about salvation as if it is a matter of love and emotion alone. Salvation is indeed a matter of love, and of course will involve our feelings as it does our mind, but it is never a matter of love alone, and not at the expense of righteousness. Salvation has to be delivered in a righteous manner.

Indeed, one of the hardest challenges any salvation way must pass is: how can a righteous God could accept us sinners and still remain righteous? But thank God, because we are not the first ones to have concerns about this. The first one to be concerned with righteousness is none other than God himself. Romans 1:17 is the critical verse for this, in which Paul says, "For in it [the gospel] the *righteousness* of God is revealed" (emphasis added).

Though at first sight there is nothing special in this sentence, when Paul says the gospel reveals the righteousness of God, he has made a breakthrough that all of us need to take heed. As stated in the preceding section, when people talk about the gospel God's righteousness is hardly touched, as if the gospel revealed only God's love. If we have to fill in the blank: "For me, the cross of Christ reveals God's . . . ," how many Christians will fill in "righteousness" and how many with "love"? I dare to say that the majority will go with "love." That is why what Paul has written is extremely important. In a sense, we must be glad that in Romans 1:17 he does not say, "For in it, the love of God is revealed," but instead mentions "the righteousness of God."

Of course, this does not mean Paul denied the gospel's display of God's love. The same Paul also said, "But God shows his love for us in that while we were still sinners, Christ died for us" (Rom 5:8). Paul did believe in the grace of God that saves sinners, including the worst one like him. But in writing Romans 1:17 the way he did, Paul has provided a great balance for Christian's understanding of the gospel.

But what does Paul mean when he says that in the gospel the righteousness of God is revealed? Keeping John 3:16 in mind, we can say that just as the love of God shines so brightly in the gospel, so is the righteousness of God brilliantly displayed in it. Here "righteousness" refers to the *attribute of God*; the gospel displays that God is righteous just as it displays that God is love.[1]

---

1. For this explanation of "righteousness" I depend largely on Moo, *Romans*, 73. More technically speaking, the term "righteousness" contains two more meanings. For Moo, besides using it to refer to an attribute of God, Paul also uses it to denote an *activity of God* and a *status given by God*. The former means "the gospel manifests the saving action of God," while the later means

This is the major unique quality of the gospel and the main point of the book in your hand. This book will insist that love and righteousness should not be put against one another. Yes, righteousness without love can be cold and merciless, but love without righteousness can only harm both the giver and the receiver of this kind of love. On the other hand, placing God's love and righteousness properly hand in hand is a powerful remedy for many Christians who are ashamed of the gospel. Have you ever noticed that those who declare that all ways of salvation must be regarded equal *always* do that solely on the ground of God's love? You will have never heard people say, "God is just. He will not have compromise with sin. His wrath is upon those who are wicked. His eternal punishment is waiting for each and every sinner. So take any way of salvation you can get, because no matter what, he (who is holy and just and righteous) will save you." This sentence makes little sense, does it not?

God must be both loving and righteous in everything he does, including when he saves us. God is the Ultimate Judge who never needs to fear answering Abraham's challenge, "Shall not the Judge of all the earth do what is just?" (Gen 18:25). Therefore, we should put the elements of justice and righteousness back into the "terms and conditions" of salvation. Christians must realize that when God saves us, he saves us in a rightful manner, and he *must* do it in a rightful manner. And the gospel is so powerful because in it God saves us according to his perfect righteousness.

The rest of the book will mostly explain how exactly God, in the gospel, saves us according to his perfect righteousness, and how this makes the gospel so powerful and irreplaceable. But before all this we must first explore what makes salvation so difficult and complex—*the sin itself!* While exploring sin will demand some chapters (four in toto), please be patient, because only after that we will be able to answer this tough question: how, *only* in the gospel, can the righteous God accept us sinners and still remain righteous?

"Paul is asserting that the gospel reveals the righteous status that is from God." Instead of weighing and choosing which one has the most perfect sense for "righteousness" in this verse, I prefer to keep all three in mind, although I emphasize more "righteousness" as referring to God's attribute, because this is the simplest meaning of this term in this passage.

V

How Many Sins Does it Take
to Put Adam out of Eden?

ONE! ONLY ONE! NOT more than one! One single sin is more than enough to put Adam and Eve out of Eden and to put all their descendants into the jeopardy that leads to their eternal condemnation. One sin . . . one sin only . . . and the whole universe was never to be the same again.

The fall of Adam and Eve is one of the most well-known tragedies. You do not have to be a Christian to be familiar with it. But its detail is probably not as popular as we think, even if we have been Christians since childhood. It's still fresh in my mind how surprised I was when a few years ago one American missionary serving in Indonesia told me that Adam must leave Eden after committing *one* sin only.[1] This simple fact amazed me and opened a whole new understanding about the seriousness of sin in the sight of our God.

As I mentioned at the very beginning, many people feel harassed when they hear Christians believe that only in Christ and nowhere else may we find salvation. But most of them have no idea how Christians arrived at this conclusion. They know the end but do not know the road. According to what I see, one of the most important missing links we need to take into account is the fact of *sin*. As long as sin is treated lightly, or worse, its existence is denied, we

1. It was the Rev. Michael Deinsmor who brought this fact to me.

will not be able to understand why there is no other way of salvation but in the blood of Jesus. On the other hand, once we realize what sin is and how serious it is in God's sight, the inimitability of Christ's sacrifice will no longer seem as strange as it does.

Therefore, we will devote some chapters to talking about sin. And we will begin with one short simple statement: sin is a *fact*. Indeed, the first and foremost thing to say about sin is that sin does exist in this world. Every time someone tells me that Christianity is full of fantasy that cannot not be proved (about God, angels, Satan, heaven, hell, etc.), neither scientifically nor in daily life, all I need to do is direct them to the fact of sin. Those who have lived long enough in this world will realize that sin is here, there, and everywhere.

Sin really exists, whether you realize it or not, and whatever names you may give to it. People may call it "lust," "unbridled desire," "immorality," "transgression," "disorder," "misbehavior," "being uncivilized," "lack of education," etc., but the basic thing is that we all realize we are not what we are supposed to be, or in Christian terms, we are sinners. Of course the Christian concept of sin is not exactly the same as all the terms above, but in the bottom line is that we know there is something wrong in this world, and in us, that needs fixing.

Indeed, sin is not only around us; it also has infected us from the very beginning of our existence. John Locke once said that every newborn baby can be compared with a sheet of blank white paper and it is up to us to write upon it. It sounds good, does it not? But is this a *fact*? While I have often heard this theory quoted by many teachers in front of classrooms or by speakers in the middle of workshops, I cannot remember if a real parent in the real world has endorsed this theory passionately, especially those with *many* kids. I suspect they will agree more with the ancient King David, who once said, "Behold, I was brought forth in iniquity, and in sin did my mother conceive me" (Ps 51:5).

Is it not a blank fact that kids can do bad things by themselves, while it takes "a whole village" to help them behave properly? You do not have to teach them how to lie; all they need is time, the opportunity, and the need. Add lack of discipline, and you will reap the fruit *abundantly*. On the other hand, it looks like a kind of magic if our kids can "automatically" be honest, especially if they know their honesty comes at a price and it's them who have to pay.

However, many people try to defend Locke and argue that people are still basically good, and what makes them bad is their neighborhood. Once again, it sounds good, does it not? But also again, is this true? We will begin to doubt it once we start to think: What exactly do they mean by "the neighborhood"? Are they not simply other people? If so, are we not actually saying, "People are basically good. What makes them bad are other people"?[2] Or, if I apply this personally to me, am I not essentially saying, "I am good. What makes me bad is you, other people! Because of you, I have become bad. It is all your fault"? Won't we agree that whoever says this is living proof of the fact of sin?

And as strange as it may seem, good religious devotees themselves are the *ultimate* proof of the fact of sin. While many of them are nice and honest, they can't help but testify that the infiltration sin is indeed so deep.

I come to this conclusion after frequently facing them in our evangelism. Living in Indonesia with so many beliefs and religions, one answer we frequently get while sharing the gospel is, "All religions are the same. They all teach what is good." People saying this want us to know that, while Christianity is not bad by itself, if you already have a religion there is no need to come to Christ.

I once met an old man in a hospital. His age was more than seventy, twice my age at that time. I can tell you that he was really a gentleman. When I entered his room, telling him that my purpose was to share the gospel, he forced himself to sit up in his sickbed. As a young Asian, I felt uncomfortable. Not only because there was a huge gap in our age, but he was also ill at that time. I tried to stop him, telling him that we could talk while he was lying, but he insisted. After he managed to find a comfortable position I started sharing the gospel, and after I was done he said to me politely, "All religions are the same."

2. I heard this for the very first time from Rev. Sutjipto Subeno.

I remember replying, "Yes, we do believe that many religions teach good things. True religions teach us to be good and honest people. But may I ask you one thing: Which one is true in your personal experience: do we obey our religion more than we disobey it, or do we disobey more often than we obey?'" His response was so similar to many people I have met: a big, wide smile. He confessed that he disobeyed more than he obeyed.

I'm telling this story because, for me, this senior religious man is a perfect example of my last point. He was more than seventy, full with experience, having eaten more salt than I have rice. Moreover, he was so gentle and I had a good time talking to him. However, while he believed his religion teaches good things, this good and religious man had to admit that even he had transgressed more often than obeyed. And this is what all religious people in the world have to admit: they disobey their religion more often than they obey it. They do not only break the rules one or two times in their life; they continually and consistently disobey what they truly believe as true, or even as divine. They display that the effect of sin is so deep.

I am not giving the technical definition of sin here but simply using illustrations from daily life to show that, whether we realize it or not, sin is a *fact*.[3] The existence of sin can't be denied and infects all human beings, even good people around us. And once we admit that sin really does exist, we are ready to face the next topic: how *serious* sin is. Why does God take such serious action in dealing with just one sin?

---

3. For a more technical and thorough explanation about the fall and the fact of sin, I would like to recommend Hoekema, *Created in God's Image*.

VI

Sin, God's Holiness, and God's Wrath

As MENTIONED IN THE previous chapter, it only took one sin to put Adam and Eve out of Eden. If we take this number literally, then from this story we can draw the hard lesson that God requires not merely good deeds, but no less than perfection: one failure is enough; you do not need to repeat it. And what is more staggering, Genesis 3 tells us that once Adam failed he and his wife had to leave Eden until they returned to dust. Is that not too demanding? Who among us dares to demand this from our children?

For us this story is hard to swallow. But we must remember that there is a difference not only between God and us, but also between Eden and our world. For sinners like us, good and evil mostly are a matter of *degree*. We do not put all people into two compartments and then label one group as "angels" and the other one as "demons." We are used to saying that Michael is better than John, or that Jane is getting worse in her morality than before. For us, in a sense, good and bad are a matter of degree, an issue of more or less, better or worse.

This is the difference: both God and Eden are holy! And for a holy God, good and evil are a matter of *separation*: we are either holy or *unholy*. There is no room in between and we cannot become both; nor can we be half a saint and half a sinner. In God's sight there is a great chasm that is fixed between holy and unholy.

While God will not put all sinners at the same level,[1] a sinner is still a sinner no matter what. Except for the redemption of the Son of God, this great chasm would remain that way for eternity. Understanding this great chasm is the key to comprehending God's reaction to the fall of Adam and Eve.

Let me give a comparison from daily life. If today we have to pay one dollar for an apple and tomorrow we have to pay two dollars for the same one, we will say that its price has been raised by 100 percent. If the day after tomorrow we have to pay three dollars for the same apple, we will say the price has once again risen, this time by 50 percent. If for some reason the apple's price reaches four dollars for each, we will say that we have to pay 33.3 percent more than the last time. Thus, the apple price is getting higher and higher, but it still can be measured by percentage. The gap is only in degree.

However, if I initially did not have to pay for the apple because the seller gave it to me for free, but now I have to pay one dollar to have it, this is no longer a matter of degree. The two are fundamentally different, with a kind of difference that cannot be measure by percentage. What percentage is the gap between zero and one? Two hundred percent? Three hundred? Or a positive infinity? We realize that this time there is a great chasm. Once we have to pay, it is no longer free, and the gap between free and price cannot be measured by percentage: it is not a matter of gradation but separation.

Similarly, once Adam fell into sin he became *unholy*. The very reason he could not stay in Eden is that Eden is a *holy* place. Before Adam ate the forbidden fruit there was no sin whatsoever in Eden. But after that very tragic moment Adam was not merely less holy, but he had become a sinner. If God had let Adam stay then Eden would have become an *unholy* place. And if God had just ignored Adam's sin then he himself would have become an *unholy* God. Adam had to leave *not* because God was too demanding. Once Adam fell into sin he had to leave because the alternative would have been unbearable.

---

1. Consider what Jesus said to Pilate: "he who delivered me over to you has the *greater* sin" (John 19:11, emphasis added).

Moreover, the same mistake may cause different consequences depending on the object of our transgression. As an example, it is a serious problem if my son bullies his friend, but he will get into much more trouble if the person receiving his jab is his schoolmaster. And he will surely get even more trouble if he makes the same offense towards his parents. These three misbehaviors are similar, but the burden of each action is totally different. If my son punches his friend we will say that he is "naughty," but if the one he punches is his teacher he is no longer simply naughty but "insolent." And if he does this horrible thing to his own parents then he has started a "rebellion." With these different names come different consequences.

Therefore, what if we transgress our God, who created us out of nothing and provides us with everything we need? The Bible calls it "sin." Sin in its very nature is a transgression against God. And because it directly attacks God himself, sin is outrageously horrible. And its consequence is "God's wrath." As Paul wrote, "For the wrath of God is revealed from heaven against all ungodliness and unrighteousness of men, who by their unrighteousness suppress the truth" (Rom 1:18). And yes, God's wrath is extremely serious.

Douglas Moo notes that the Greek philosophers rejected the idea of a God who pours out his wrath because, for them, this idea of an angry God could not be matched with "an enlightened understanding of the deity."[2] Also according to Moo, "The second-century Christian heretic Marcion omitted 'of God' in v. 18, and many others since would like to omit the verse altogether."[3] However, Moo cannot be more correct in saying, "God's wrath is an aspect of God's person." God could not remain God if he is passive and does nothing against the sin cheerfully performed in front of him. According to Nygren, "As long as God is God, He cannot behold with indifference that His creation is destroyed and his holy will trodden underfoot. Therefore he meets sin with his mighty and annihilating reaction."[4]

Could we say that today the idea of God's wrath has finally become more popular? I dare not. Even today we love to have God

2. Moo, *Romans*, 99.

3. Ibid., 99.

4. Quoted in ibid., 100.

without wrath, a Santa Claus without his elves that punish the bad kids. However, our popular concept of God as a Higher Being who knows only to love has blurred our perspective. Because we see our God is so full of compassion, we used to think that to transgress against him is not a very serious matter. Like a popular quote has said, "I love to sin, God loves to forgive. What a wonderful arrangement." This erroneous understanding makes us fear others, and even the devil, much more than we fear our Lord.

Because we are used to thinking that God of the Bible is full of compassion and slow to anger, we tend to forget that this same holy book also says that "the Lord will by no means clear the guilty" (Nah 1:3). Paul in Romans 1:18–32 gives us a vivid picture about how serious sin is and how God will react against it. From these verses we can learn that our God is not only able to pour his wrath, but also to pour it out heavily. I agree with Schiller, who said, "The history of the world is the judgment of the world."[5] As sin is a reality, God's wrath is also a solid fact that can be seen here, there, and everywhere. Our merciful God is indeed "a consuming fire" (Heb 12:29).

However, can we see God's wrath as clearly as we recognize sin in our daily life? When I ask this question on some occasions, many affirm that an earthquake at one place or a tsunami at another continent has proved that God is furious toward the wickedness of human being. We used to relate natural disasters with God's wrath upon our transgressions. But while this kind of answer may not totally miss the mark, we must use it with great caution.

First of all, after Adam's fall, the Bible says that all of nature was cursed (Gen 3:17) and that "the whole creation has been groaning together in the pains of childbirth until now" (Rom 8:22). So while it could be right to say that *all* natural disasters are caused by human sin, we have to be careful *not* to say that a particular natural disaster at a particular place is caused by the particular sins of the particular people who live in that place. That kind of statement only shows the blindness of our own wickedness. Who would dare

5. Quoted in ibid., 101.

say that we are better than those who live in Banda Aceh or Japan when the tsunami hit them?

Interestingly, when Paul explores God's wrath already revealed from heaven in Romans 1:18–32, he is *not* referring to natural disasters. Not even one time does Paul point his finger to an earthquake or to a big flood. Paul simply has other things in mind—things that are more ordinary but are much more solid proofs for God's wrath than any calamities that have ever happened, either in his time or our time. Take a closer look at these verses:

> For although they knew God, they did not honor him as God or give thanks to him, but they became futile in their thinking, and their foolish hearts were darkened. Claiming to be wise, they became fools, and exchanged the glory of the immortal God for images resembling mortal man and birds and animals and creeping things. *Therefore* God gave them up in the lusts of their hearts to impurity, to the dishonoring of their bodies among themselves. (Rom 1:21–24, emphasis added)

> And *since* they did not see fit to acknowledge God, God gave them up to a debased mind to do what ought not to be done. They were filled with all manner of unrighteousness, evil, covetousness, malice. They are full of envy, murder, strife, deceit, maliciousness. They are gossips, slanderers, haters of God, insolent, haughty, boastful, inventors of evil, disobedient to parents, foolish, faithless, heartless, ruthless. (Rom 1:28–31, emphasis added)

Through all these verses, Paul is not connecting God's wrath to natural disasters but to *human sins*. He is talking about lust, envy, gossip, boastfulness, foolishness, faithlessness, etc. For Paul, God's punishment for human wickedness is in binding us to more and more sin. What a surprise! It is, in a sense, quite easy to relate God's wrath with natural disasters, but how could gossip or envy be a kind of punishment? When Jonah came to Nineveh and called out, "Yet forty days, and Nineveh shall be overthrown!" (Jonah 3:4), they got the point. But what if Jonah told them instead, "Yet forty days, and you will find more and more gossipers among you!"? Would they also get the point and then repent as wholeheartedly?

"Shall be overthrown" is by any means a serious discipline and a terrible judgment. But it is not directly clear how being faithless and boastful can be put at the same level.

However, a deeper reflection reveals that it not only makes sense that more sin is a serious judgment for our unrighteousness, but it is also actually hard to find any catastrophes that might weigh more severely than sin. Consider this: how many people have you ever known of who killed themselves because they were so desperate after an earthquake destroyed their house and everything in it? Can you mention people who have committed suicide because of natural disasters? You maybe can, or maybe cannot, but no matter what, you will need time looking for that.

Now consider this: have you ever heard of husbands or wives who committed suicide because their soulmate left them for a younger partner? Have you ever heard of people who hanged themselves because they were betrayed by someone they trusted or because their small company was been mercilessly destroyed by a bigger one? How many tears have been poured by parents because of their insolent kids? How many kids live with permanent damage because of their parents's divorce? I believe that you will nod almost *automatically*.

All these are enough to explain why Paul chose this "moral evil" to show that God has poured his wrath. This passage opens our eyes to the horror of sin. It does not only corrupt nature but also destroy human being themselves. What makes our life so difficult is not only cursed nature, but also and especially sin and much more sin. Greediness is one of the cruelest enemies of humankind, as it is unfaithfulness. However, this passage also displays that God is able to pour his wrath even to this extent. He is able not only to bring natural disaster on earth, but also to deliver people to more and more sin. While his mercy is abundantly rich, his wrath upon sin is imminent and unforgettable.

As a summary, sin is very serious: it is a transgression against the Creator himself, a willing and full-hearted rebellion of ungrateful creatures to their merciful Creator and gracious Provider. And God reacts to sin as a "consuming fire" (Heb 12:29).

VII

Our Good Neighbors and
What About Those Who Never Heard?

PLEASE ALLOW ME TO introduce a friend of mine whose integrity I truly admire. We went to the same university, had the same classes, and got involved in the same campus organization. To be honest, I have hardly found any other student with an integrity as honorable as his. First of all, he was totally upright in class; he never cheated or did anything like that. I remember once he came to class a bit late. When he wanted to sign the attendance list, he found that another student had already done that for him, thereby forging a false signature. What he did was erase his friend's signature and then put his own signature on it!

But surprisingly, in spite of his uprightness, this friend of mine was one of the most popular students on our campus. And that is not because he was a sports star with a very athletic posture, nor because he was blessed with a very good-looking face. The reason why people liked to be his friend, although he was so upright, was because he was very helpful. No student would dare ask for answers from him during exams. But before or after an exam he was always willing to help others with difficulties in understanding. Besides, he was a leader in our campus organization and a very funny guy, who often made fun of himself.

But as the final remark, he was *not* a Christian, and was even a bit cynical about religion. And I think it can be justified if I describe him as an atheist, or at least an agnostic. I tried to evangelize him once and he declined it politely.

The question is clear: does this kind of guy need Christ? Does he deserve eternal punishment just because he is ignorant about the Savior? And the bigger problem is that he is not alone. There are many others who, while probably not as remarkable as he, still deserve to be called "good neighborhood"; many of them are good husbands, responsible wives, honest workers, and diligent children. The problem is that they just do not think they need Christ.

To this add the fact that while Christianity is the first world religion in the history of humankind,[1] and still the biggest religion today, and not growing weary,[2] we are still a minority compared to those who are non-Christians. To make matters even worse, how about those who never had an opportunity to listen to the gospel during their lifetime? What about our ancestors who already passed away even before Christ was born?

Put all these questions within the framework of our last chapter, and we will have no doubt that even this Mr. Nice Guy needs to be saved by the blood of Jesus, because even he is not *perfectly* good. But still, to think that he deserves *eternal* punishment will make many of us feel uneasy. Therefore, even after scrutinizing the last chapter, it is fully understood if some of us still find it difficult to digest that salvation is only in Christ. Not because we cannot explain it, but more because we find it difficult to swallow.

All these realities demand more reflection, but first thing first: sin is a tragedy! It is wrong to think that Christians feel comfortable about the prospect of hell for non-Christians. No, we do not. If hell were an easy topic, we wouldn't find theologians who argue for universal salvation, nor those who embrace annihilationism.[3] It is not my purpose to discuss these views, but at the bottom line,

---

1. Neill, *History,* 473.

2. According to Jenkins, "Some 2.1 billion Christians were alive in 2005, about one-third of the planetary population" (*Next Christendom*, 2).

3. Annihilationism is the view that people outside Christ will perish at their death, instead of being punished eternally in hell.

thinking seriously about people who would be damned eternally is difficult, to say the least.

On the other hand, if we do believe that there is God, and that this God is the holy and righteous God of the Bible, then Christians *must* talk about the reality of hell. Those who argue for universalism or annihilationism must ask whether they indeed realize that this is a matter of life and death. Do they realize that what is at stake here is not only our reputation, nor simply our good feeling about the fate of others, nor even our peace of mind, but we are dealing with the very souls of those who are lost?

Therefore we should not talk about hell easily, nor should we diminish it lightly. And this is especially true for Christians because Christianity is the only religion that gives no second chance after death. All other beliefs give room for a second chance; something can still be done for the deceased: we can pray for them, "give" something to them, do something good on their behalf, etc. But in Christianity, the Bible clearly states that "it is appointed for man to die once, and after that comes judgment" (Heb 9:27). That is why we should talk about sin and the judgment of God seriously and carefully.

As we already discussed in previous chapter, the same mistake can have different weight depending on the person to whom the mistake is made. If my son punches his friend, he deserves detention. But if he punches his teacher, a mere detention is not enough. Now if he dares to do that to me or to his mother or grandmother, the story will be totally different. This is exactly why sin is so serious. It is directed against none other than God himself.

But even more than that, we must remember that counting sin is different from simple mathematics. Imagine a father who not only believes that to lie is wrong but also constantly warns his kids not to lie. What if he himself lies? Will his wrongdoing become less or more serious? On the one hand, to warn our kids not to lie is a good thing, is it not? But on the other hand, sin is not a mathematical calculation in which one good minus one bad brings us back to zero. All of us will agree that a father who insists that his kids should not lie and punishes them when they lie commits a more grievous misconduct when he himself lies.

The moral of the story is of course not that parents should not teach their kids moral lessons; it is to show that, as weird as it is, being a good person can actually make our transgression more serious. Please note that being good in some areas *cannot* cover our failure in other areas. As a comparison, a doctor who had succeeded in saving hundreds of lives through surgeries cannot run from a sentence when one of his patients passes away during a surgery because of his negligence.[4] This reminds us of what the Letter of James says: "For whoever keeps the whole law but fails in one point has become accountable for all of it" (2:10).

We can say a similar thing for religious people. On the one hand, we must admire those who are really devoted to what they believe. On the other hand, the more religious someone is, then, in a sense, the more evil his or her transgression is. Each of us has a conscience. That is why we cannot excuse our wrongdoing, whether we are atheist or religious. However, religious people have more than their conscience: they have rules and instructions that they believe have come to them from God himself. Therefore, when sinning, they transgress not only against their conscience but also their heart and mind, because they transgress against what they believe in their heart to be the holy book, which clearly informs their mind about what is right and what is wrong. And this is exactly what Paul the apostle already realized almost two thousand years ago when he wrote, "For while we were living in the flesh, our sinful passions, aroused by the law, were at work in our members to bear fruit for death. . . . For sin, seizing an opportunity through the commandment, deceived me and through it killed me" (Rom 7:5, 11). Sin is much more serious, dangerous, and subtle than we ever thought.

But what about those who never heard of the gospel? If the fact of hell is as serious as we have discussed above, what about so many people who never had a chance to receive Christ? Again, we must not treat this issue lightly. But as hard as it is, still it must

---

4. I have heard this illustration from Ivan Adi Raharjo.

be stated that God has no obligation to save even one of us. There is no injustice when someone who never heard about the gospel must bear God's punishment *because of their transgressions.* We must not forget that when we sin, we sin deliberately. Rarely does someone compel us to sin. And more often than not, we already know that what we are going to do is wrong, do we not? All of us have a conscience. When we make a mistake consciously and calculatingly, how can we think that we still have a right to demand that God save us?

Therefore, according to Paul, "For by grace you have been saved through faith. And this is not your own doing; it is the gift of God" (Eph 2:8). This means we get what we do not deserve; it is merely the goodness of God. If we are saved, we are saved by grace. If we are condemned, we are justly condemned, because of our own sins and transgressions. This is not because God wants to take all credit and cast a bad light upon us; it is simply the way it is.

One illustration will make this even clearer.[5] When two drivers drive over the speed limit, crash their cars, and injure themselves badly, there is no one to be blamed but themselves. However, the first one was driving in the midst of the city. A good doctor happened to see his accident and gave him immediate help, which saved his life. Unfortunately, the second driver was in the middle of nowhere. When help came it was already too late. To whom must we give credit in the first case? The doctor or the driver? And who must be blamed for the second one? Again, the doctor or the driver? I do not think I need to provide answers for these questions.

Thus, while we are not supposed to rejoice for those who do not have an opportunity to receive God's grace, it is a mistake to blame God for this. It is also a mistake to deny the gospel as the only way of salvation just because a lot of people have never heard about it. I fully realize that even after all the explanations above, the fact of eternal punishment because of sin is still hard to swallow. But as hard as it is, we do nothing good in denying it. The

5. I know this illustration for the first time from Rev. Gatot Setiabudi (Dec.).

solution is not in rejecting the gospel but in sharing it with those who have never heard about it, in humility instead of in arrogance, and to pray that God will work in the hearts of those who hear it.

Regarding my friend whom I told you about at the beginning of this chapter, I met him a couple of times after we both finished our studies. We even once talked about the gospel during our lunch. However, up to now he has still decided not to become a believer. But it is my constant longing that someday God will open his heart, and he will see the true hope of the gospel.

VIII

The Significance of Sin and of a Savior

ONE UNFORGETTABLE SCENE IN the first *Matrix* movie is when Neo decides to swallow the red pill given to him by Morpheus instead of the blue one. The red pill is the pill of reality. After Neo devours it, he is able to "wake up" and see the world as it really is. How shocked he is, realizing that the world he used to know is no more than dreams programmed by the mainframe, while the real world is not only totally different but also fully unlikeable! Those who cannot stand facing reality are represented by Chiper, who betrays his friends so that the mainframe's agents can put him back in his dream capsule and give him the particular kind of dream he loves to have.

Why should we take our discussion of sin as meticulously as in these previous chapters? Because sin is a *fact*. We may hate this fact, but we need to wake up and face it. We may love to talk about God's mercy for hours and feel encouraged after that, but until we understand the fact of sin, its seriousness, and God's wrath upon it, we may not know what we are talking about; we are just dreaming up our own idea about God.

An apologist once said that if he has got sixty minutes for conversation with someone about the gospel, he will use fifty minutes of it talking about the bad news, and then for the remaining ten minutes he will talk about the good news itself. The reason is that people who don't know the real situation will not take heed when they listen to the gospel. How wise he is!

Not really understanding what is at stake, many people choose religion with an attitude not too different from choosing fast food restaurants or popular soft drinks. Sometimes when we want to go to McDonald's, we can easily end up at Burger King or Wendy's. Or when we go to a restaurant and order Coke, we rarely complain if the waiter serves Pepsi or Dr. Pepper instead—this is just a matter of soda anyway. The fact is that many people choose religion with a very similar attitude, and this is because they have no idea about the true weight of religion.

Once while in an airport waiting for a flight, I met someone working for the government. After a short conversation, he learned that I am a pastor and we started talking about religion. He told me that he is a religious man, although not a Christian, and he affirmed that religion is so important *for a good society*. I can agree that true religion is a great benefit for any society, and truly religious people are a blessing for those who live around them. But what troubled me during our conversation was that for this man religion matter not because it has to do with the afterlife, but merely because it can help us control society. For him, without religion it is harder to control people, and that is why religion matters.

How similar is this with Dan Brown's *DaVinci Code*. In the end of the book we read that the Catholic faith is a hoax. The definitive proof for it has been buried for ages, but is finally discovered. But instead of releasing it to the public, the hero of the novel, Robert Langdon, prefers to keep it hidden. The reason is that, although it is false, Catholic faith has at least brought stability to the world. This stability would be threatened if millions of believers found out that what they believe to be true turns out to be fake.

Dan Brown is not alone, nor is the government employee that I met at the airport. All these are simply so postmodern. Different from modernism, postmodernism will not imagine the world without religion. It affirms religion as its affirm the spirituality of human beings. That is why it does not wish to vanquish religion, something that some modernism tried to do adamantly (and failed miserably). What postmodernism wants is bracketing or taming religions; it loves to be served by religions that cannot unleash their true power. And the best way to put a religion in jail is to make it focus only on current issues instead of eternal ones.

That is why, while the next chapters of this book may stand as the core of the whole, they must be built upon the previous ones. Those who are still unconvinced about our desperate situation under God's wrath and the tyranny of sin will very probably find our following discussions too "technical." If all of us are fine already, or if God so loves the world that he will save the whole of it no matter what, then why should we scrutinize how and why God must save us through the death of his Son, Jesus Christ? Why must we analyze Christ's work in detail if any work or any way will bring us to God?

On the contrary, once we grasp that our eternal damnation under God's wrath because of sin is a real thing, then Christianity will genuinely matter. Choosing religion is no longer similar to choosing a fast food restaurant or a soft drink brand; it is more like choosing a surgeon or a lawyer in a very critical situation. When you realize that your illness is dreadfully critical or your case is terribly serious, you will not go to any random doctor or lawyer; you will painstakingly choose the right one. You will get so upset if, instead of the doctor or the lawyer that you prefer, the one who meets you and takes your case is an assistant or colleague. Considering your desperate situation, you will demand to have exactly the one that you prefer—no more, no less. Moreover, you will scrutinize all the details and make sure to follow all the advice as rigorous as possible; nothing will be too technical to you.

That is why the following part of this book must be read with the previous ones as the foreground, not merely as the background. Sin is so serious that even one drop of it is enough to put all of humankind into trouble. God's fury is upon us sinners, and the bowl of his wrath is ready to be poured out unto us. We find a hopeless situation.

But what exactly can God do to save us? Basically, there are three options. The first is simply ignoring our transgression: God accepts us without taking our sins seriously. But as we previously saw, this option fundamentally does not exist. If there is God, then he must be just; an unjust God is simply an oxymoron.

The second way is to give us holy instructions about how to get into heaven. But we also know that the sin in us will turn these holy instructions to be dead to us. Once we know these instructions, our desire as sinners is to do precisely the opposite. As Paul told us two thousand years ago, "It was sin, producing death in me through what is good, in order that sin might be shown to be sin, and through the commandment might become sinful beyond measure" (Rom 7:13). In the face of sin, these good commandments are totally powerless.

Hence, if God cannot just forgive us, and it is not enough to send us the recipe for salvation, then God must take on the whole burden by himself; he must provide all that it takes to save us. Because it takes much more than a forgiver or a guru in order to save us, God must provide a savior that will not only tell us what to do but also be able to take our burden of sin upon himself. And this savior was provided on Christmas night, when the Son of God became man to save us.

God had to become man because this is the only way he could provide salvation for humankind. Only this kind of savior can bear the heaviness of God's wrath upon sin! And only when this savior drank the cup of God's wrath to the last drop could *shalom* between God and humankind be regained (cf. Rom 1:18 and Rom 5:1). All depends on a savior!

Many people today will be reluctant to believe that the death of God's Son is to appease his Father's wrath. But we must remember that God's anger against sin is a holy anger. For God to punish sin is jut as for a righteous judge to punish crime; he simply has to do it. There is nothing cruel in it; it is but all justice. God's wrath upon sinners is not a matter of God releasing his burnout without thinking carefully and later regretting it; this is a matter of God's very nature against the fact of sin. Furthermore, to appease God's wrath is not similar to us humans trying desperately to make another human calm down. To appease God's wrath means taking the price of sin on oneself and paying it fully until no debt is left.

Only after that can God forgive sinners without sacrificing his holy righteousness.

Therefore this savior can't be just anyone who is willing to die, but must be someone *worthy enough* to die in exchange for sinners; plus he must be *powerful enough* to devour the wrath of God. And this can be found only in Jesus, the true God that became the true man. And we will devote our next discussions to understanding him and the work that he did to save us.

IX

The Savior That We Have:
Fully God and Fully Man

NOT TOO MANY PEOPLE will care about the number of Muhammad's or Siddhartha's brothers. Nor many will bother about whether they were the eldest or the youngest sibling. And the fact is, this will have no impact whatsoever to the existence of Islam or Buddhism.

But how different Christianity is! There have been hundreds years of debates about whether James and Jude were Jesus' brothers or *step*brothers. Also, thousands of pages have been used in answering if Jesus was older or younger than them both. However, the most staggering thing is the fact that Jesus must be the oldest among his brothers and sisters or else all Christianity will collapse![1] Similarly, Jesus must be a Jew, must be born from the tribe of Judah, must have died on the cross, and his tomb must be empty, or else there is no biblical Christianity.

No other religion has been so attached to its founder or leader as much as Christianity is to Jesus Christ. Even the smallest fact about Jesus matters that much. We cannot change our portrait of

1. This is of course assuming that James and Judas were both sons of Mary and therefore the true brothers, and not only stepbrothers, of Jesus. Those who feel that I have made an overstatement must remember that if Jesus is the second or third son of Mary, that would mean Mary had not been a virgin when she was "found to be with child from the Holy Spirit" (Matt 1:18). And if that was the case, then Jesus was born in sin like the rest of us and cannot be the second Adam. Therefore, Jesus *must* be the first child of Mary.

Jesus without changing the whole picture of Christianity. All these historical facts about Jesus are important to make Christianity as it is. Christ is not only the founder or the sustainer of Christianity; he is the *cornerstone!* Christianity rises and falls with its Christ.

In Christianity's scheme of salvation, Christ is also the center. All we have said about a powerful and righteous salvation is only possible if Christ is what he is in the Bible. In this chapter we will discuss the nature of our Savior and what he has done to save all who believe. We are not going to discuss every aspect of Christ; it would take a whole book. What we will see is that Christ is fully God and fully man. Understanding these two natures of Christ will help us affirming why in him God can save us fully and righteously.

Jesus: Fully God

First of all, Jesus must be God, or he is not able to provide the righteous way of salvation. If Jesus is less than God—if he is just a saint, an angel, or even a god with a small "g," like what the Jehovah's Witnesses would like us to believe—then there is no way we can be saved by his blood. No mere human can be a savior. All of us, including saints, are under the debt of sin, and the one who is himself full of debt is not qualified to pay other people's debts. Therefore, we can't redeem either ourselves or others.

But what about the angels? Beside the fallen ones, all angels are holy, are they not? What about the cherubim and the seraphim who stand in the face of God? Why can't they become a ransom for us? Is it because they are not willing? Or is it because they are not able, even if they are willing? According to Revelation 5, the last one is the answer: they are not worthy enough for that. In that chapter John says, "And I saw a mighty angel proclaiming with a loud voice, 'Who is worthy to open the scroll and break its seals?' . . . And no one in heaven or on earth or under the earth was able to open the scroll or to look into it" (5:2–3). This fact crushes John because he knows that the scroll is the scroll of salvation, and as long as it cannot be opened all its content is void. Revelation 4–5 records the heavenly scene in which we meet "twenty-four elders"

45

(4:4), "four living creatures," which are seraphim (4:5), and "many angels, numbering myriads of myriads and thousands of thousands" (5:11). But *no one* is able to open the scroll! No wonder John is devastated. Who then can save humankind?

But one of the elders comes and says to John, "Weep no more; behold, the Lion of the tribe of Judah, the Root of David, has conquered, so that he can open the scroll and its seven seals." Right after that John saw "a Lamb . . . as though it had been slain . . . went and took the scroll from the right hand of him who was seated on the throne" (5:6–7). This lamb is Jesus, about whom the host of heaven sings a new song: "Worthy are you to take the scroll and to open its seals, for you were slain, and by your blood you ransomed people for God from every tribe and language and people and nation . . . " (5:9). Thus, among the myriads of myriads and thousands of thousands of the host of heaven, only Jesus can open the scroll and be the redeemer.

Thus, a savior can't be just anyone who is willing to die, nor are angels able to open the scroll of salvation, no matter how high their rank is. A true savior cannot be just *a* god either, as according to the Jehovah's Witnesses. Jesus must be God in the fullest sense of the word, or his blood is not able to "ransom people for God from every tribe and language and people and nation."

I once met the Jehovah's Witnesses district leader. During our conversation he kept saying that Protestantism and the Jehovah's Witnesses are basically not different. He insisted that we are almost identical. Honestly, this tempted me to ask why they are trying so hard to "evangelize" us if both are so indistinguishable from each other. But instead I answered him, "Please forgive me. I must say that we are not same. If you are right, then we are in trouble. And if we are right, then you will be in trouble." Now, on second thought I think it is better to say, "If we are right, then you are in trouble. If you are right, then *both of us* will be in trouble!"

This statement may sound controversial. They, as we, believe in Jesus as the only savior of the world. They also believe in Jesus as the creator of the universe. And of course, they will not reject that Jesus is, in a sense, god. But here the tricky thing comes up:

they believe that Jesus is *a god*, but not *God*. But, one may ask, why bother? If the difference between Protestantism and the Jehovah's Witnesses is only a matter of one capital letter, then is it not true that they are basically identical? No, it is absolutely not! Like what I noted above, a small shift about Christ is enough to disrupt all of Christianity, and this one is a clear example of it. For them, Jesus is god with a small "g" because they believe that even though he is the creator of the whole universe, he himself is created by Jehovah. Thus, for the Jehovah's Witnesses, Jesus is the created creator and therefore god with a small "g"; Jehovah is the one and only God, in the fullest sense of the word.

Now if they were right, we would surely have a huge problem. First, if Jesus is less than the real God, then we are no different from the idol worshipers: we worship someone who is actually not God himself. If Jesus was created, then for two thousand years Christianity has worshiped, and has taught others to worship, a creature. Albeit, it could be argued that Christ is a much more sophisticated creation than the rest of us, but no matter how great a creature he is, he is still a created one.

Second, we *and* they must doubt the love of Jehovah. In John 3:16 we read, "For God so loved the world, that he gave his only Son, that whoever believes in him should not perish but have eternal life." Is it not too much to praise God's love as John 3:16 if the fact was that God gave not his only Son, but his most valuable *creation*? If Jesus was created then he is not only less than God, he is also not God's Son in the fullest sense of the word. At best, Jesus is the son of God as we are the sons of God, without any qualitative difference. Then the whole John 3:16 must be read, "For God so loved the world, that he gave his *most precious creature*."

Of course, according to the Jehovah's Witnesses, Jesus is not merely a creation like the rest of us because he is the one who created us; thus he is special indeed. But the fact is that, no matter how special Jesus is, he is hardly God's Son in the fullest sense of the word, and he is also hardly God's *only* Son. If God can make Jesus out of nothing, how difficult is it for him to create two or three or more of Jesus? And if this is the case, how great is God's love in giving Jesus to die for us? Who truly deserves the credit? God the Creator? Or Jesus the created one? Only if Jesus is God's Son in the truest meaning of the word can we praise *both* the Father and the Son: "To him who sits on the throne and to the Lamb be blessing and honor and glory and might forever and ever!" (Rev 5:13). We must praise the Son because he sacrificed himself in our place. And we must hail the Father because he gave his only beloved Son.

But third—and here comes the critical point—if they turn out to be right then we *and* they will have no hope to be saved by Jesus, even though he already died for us at the cross. Even though the Jehovah's Witnesses believe that Jesus is the only Savior, their version of Jesus is neither powerful nor precious enough to save us: his sacrifice is not be powerful enough to transform death unto life (Rom 5:21), nor precious enough to ransom us from the futile ways inherited from our forefathers (1 Pet 1:19–20).

To understand this, we need to start by reminding ourselves that God's anger is not equal with human rage, nor his forgiveness with human remorse. Our indignation toward our sons or daughters could disappear all at once if we got news that they were just in a fatal accident. Our human emotion can change drastically in a very short moment. Once we see them lying helpless in a hospital room, we will forget all the wrongdoing they have committed. But redemption is *not* like this.

On the contrary, forgiving sin is not only a matter of God's emotion, but also of God's righteousness. This means the quality of the ransom matters. The Savior's blood cannot just be ordinary blood. It must have such a value and power that when it is being poured out all who believe can be justified surely and righteously. It is not because God is hard to satisfy, but because he is righteous. As a righteous God, he must demand an equal ransom for every sin that we have committed. The righteous judge should not demand more, but also cannot demand less. The alternative is that we have no righteous way of salvation, but only an easy one, as if God considers the ransom of Christ worthy and powerful enough just because he wants to, without any objective ground.

But if this is the case, why then even bother to provide ransom? If God could justify us simply because there is someone who wants to shed his blood for us, no matter what value the sacrifice has, then surely he can justify us with no sacrifice at all. All he needs to do is to close his eyes to our sins and embrace us lovingly no matter who we are. Now if this is not the case, then for Jesus to save me he must be able to ransom *all* sins of mine, which are many more than the hairs on my head. He must pay it fully or there is no salvation. If, for the sake of argument, he paid for all but one of my sins, then I would still be condemned no matter what.

It is time for Christians to realize that the task of the Savior is extremely daunting. Christ must bear the heaviness of *all* my sins to be able to save *one* person, which is me. And for Jesus to be a ransom for all the people of God, he must shed his blood for *each and every* sin of *each and every* person of God. How heavy is the burden that the Savior must bear!

The ground for this can be found in Romans 5. In verse 15 Paul says, "But the free gift is not like the trespass. For if many died through one man's trespass, much more have the grace of God and the free gift by the grace of that one man Jesus Christ abounded for many." In this verse Paul is comparing the first and the second Adam. He pronounces that the grace of God through the second Adam abounds much more than the death through the first Adam's trespass. However, mathematically speaking, those who perish because of Adam's transgression are much more than those who are saved because of Christ's obedience, are they not? Then in what sense can Paul say that "the free gift is not like the trespass"?

Romans 5:16 provides the answer: "And the free gift is not like the result of that one man's sin. For the judgment following *one* trespass brought condemnation, but the free gift following *many* trespasses brought justification" (emphasis added). It takes only *one* sin to bring all people to damnation, but to save even one person, it is not enough to redeem only one sin. Therefore, quantitatively speaking, there are a lot more people damned because of Adam than those who are saved because of Christ. But qualitatively speaking, the power of Christ's obedience surpasses the power of Adam's transgression.

The miraculous thing is only with one act of sacrifice Christ is able to wash away so many sins of so many believers. According to the Bible, he did not need "to suffer repeatedly since the foundation of the world. But as it is, he has appeared once for all at the end of the ages to put away sin by the sacrifice of himself" (Heb 9:26). One sacrifice, once for all, is enough to redeem all believers across the ages: he "entered once for all into the holy places, not by means of the blood of goats and calves but by means of his own blood, thus securing an eternal redemption" (Heb 9:12).

Therefore, his sacrifice must be extremely precious and powerful or the problem will arise immediately: is it *righteous* for God to justify *millions* of *sinners* across the ages, just because *one* person *once* died for them? This is a very critical question. The answer cannot be an easy yes or an easy no, but it depends on the *quality* of the Savior who become the ransom for many: for *one* sacrifice to be enough to pay for all debt of all believers, this sacrifice must be precious beyond measure. Only in that case can grace, instead of injustice, be poured out.

As a comparison, let me give an illustration. If my son played with his friend who brought hundreds pieces of diamond-shaped glass, and because of my son's carelessness all them fell into the sewer and disappeared, what I am supposed to do as a father? If instead of replacing hundreds of glass diamonds, I simply give ten glass diamonds to my son's friend—because that is all that I have— and after that send him home, then I am indeed unfair, am I not? But if I give one *real* diamond, am I still being unfair? Or would you agree that I am not only fair, but unbelievable graceful? The value of one diamond simply cannot be compared to hundreds of glass diamonds.

We should not stretch an illustration too much, but in similarity with that, only because Jesus is the God that became man can his blood and his sacrifice be as precious and as powerful as that. Jesus's blood is valuable beyond measure. As Peter said, "You were ransomed from the futile ways inherited from your forefathers, not with perishable things such as silver or gold, but with *the precious* blood of Christ, like that of a lamb without blemish or spot" (1 Pet 1:19–20, emphasis added).

Therefore, if the Jehovah's Witnesses are right, then there is no salvation—not only for us but also for them. Anything less than this precious blood of Christ makes our salvation doubtful. No other blood is precious enough; no other sacrifice is powerful enough. Only with the precious blood of Christ can God forgive sinners while maintaining his holy righteousness. Jesus must be God in the fullest sense of the word, or there is no righteous way of salvation.

Jesus: Fully Man

Now, after affirming Jesus as God in the fullest sense of the word, we also need to comprehend that Jesus is a human being exactly like you and me, only without sin. In Jesus we find true God, who emptied himself to become true man, and that is why he can be a true mediator between God and man. As Paul has declared:

> . . . Christ Jesus, who, though he was in the form of God, did not count equality with God a thing to be grasped, but emptied himself, by taking the form of a servant, being born in the likeness of men. Being found in human form, he humbled himself by becoming obedient to the point of death, even death on a cross. (Phil 2:5–8)

This pericope is unique. In it we can see that the Bible sees Jesus as both no less than God and no less than man. First of all, Paul said that Jesus is *in the form of God*. What does this mean? Here I do not have any intention to quote a definition from a Greek lexicon or theological dictionary for the meaning of "form," but I want to assert that if the meaning of "form" in this verse is anything less than "being God" in the fullest sense of the word, then Paul's argument crumbles at once. In the context of this letter, Paul makes this statement because he wants the Philippians to learn humility from the grand example of Jesus. But if Jesus was less than God, then to say that he "did not count equality with God a thing to be grasped" is *not* an example of humility; this is but an example of great arrogance.

What if I said, "I do not count my equality with Abraham Lincoln a thing to be grasped and, because of that, you do not have to honor me like you honor him"? Would I be humble? Or would you directly, and rightly, ask, "Who wants to honor you like Lincoln, anyway?" Only if I were a president in the status and capacity of Lincoln could this statement be an example of humility. But if in fact I'm not, there must be something wrong with me to make this kind of statement. Similarly, if Jesus is not God, then to say that he "did not count equality with God a thing to be grasped" is not to praise his humility, but to show blasphemy. Only if Jesus is himself God, in the fullest sense of the word, can he forfeit his right as God, because only then has he such a right. Thus, in these verses Paul is stating that Jesus is God in the fullest sense of the word.

But what does "empty himself" mean? I still have no intention to copy pages from a theological dictionary, but whatever it means, it cannot mean less than this: as Jesus is the real God, he is also a real man. And this is the core of the righteous way of salvation: we are saved by a Savior who is the God that became man.[2]

But why must things become as complicated as this? While it is already clear, I hope, that we must be saved by God himself, why is it really necessary for God to become a man? The basic answer is: *the one who is able to bear God's punishment is God himself; the one who must be punished is human.* Therefore a savior *must* be fully God and fully man so that, as God, he can endure whatever it takes to save us and that, as man, he can sit in our place to receive the punishment because of our sin. Commenting on the sacrifice of the Old Testament, the writer of the Hebrew said, "For it is impossible for the blood of bulls and goats to take away sins"

2. In the language of the Council of Chalcedon, Jesus is "to be acknowledged in two natures, inconfusedly, unchangeably, indivisibly, inseparably; the distinction of natures being by no means taken away by the union, but rather the property of each nature being preserved, and concurring in one Person and one Subsistence, not parted or divided into two persons, but one and the same Son, and only begotten God, the Word, the Lord Jesus Christ."

(10:4). The author declares that a human being cannot be replaced by bulls or by goats; a human being must be redeemed by human being. That is why God must become man.

Jesus must fully obey God as a man. The first Adam had failed to obey, and all humanity collapsed with his failure. If humankind wants to have any hope again, the second Adam must pass the test and then give himself as a worthy sacrifice. Therefore, being found in human form, Jesus must display perfect obedience, and then die at the cross in our place. Throughout the New Testament the theme of Jesus's obedience is of extreme importance. And this theme of the total obedience of the Savior is consistent with the Old Testament:

> All we like sheep have gone astray; we have turned—every one—to his own way; and the LORD has laid on him the iniquity of us all. He was oppressed, and he was afflicted, yet he opened not his mouth; like a lamb that is led to the slaughter, and like a sheep that before its shearers is silent, so he opened not his mouth. (Isa 53:6–7).

Anyone who wants to take away our sins must prove himself worthy of it; that is, he must be able to do God's will to the full extent of it and must not fail, even once.[3] Only after that is he able to offer himself as a ransom.[4] And according to Hebrews this is exactly what Christ has done:

3. The sinlessness of Christ is most important. And this is the very reason he must be born from a virgin. Interestingly, while the Qur'an also records the virgin birth of *Isa Al'masih* (their name for Jesus), only in the Bible do we know the *reason* for it. Luke records the conversation between the angel and Mary: "The Holy Spirit will come upon you, and the power of the Most High will overshadow you; therefore the child to be born will be called holy—the Son of God" (1:35). This makes sure that baby Jesus is not contaminated by sin at all. He was most holy when he was born. He never sinned up until his death. That is why God does not abandon Jesus's soul to Hades, because he cannot let his "Holy One see corruption" (Acts 2:27).

4. According to O'Brien (*Hebrews*, 351), "His mission is his complete preoccupation with doing God's will. His obedience anticipates the important conclusion that the offering of Christ is the sacrifice that God desired. Christ's fulfilling of God's will is the reason that his sacrifice effect what the animal sacrifices under the old covenant could not achieve."

> For we do not have a high priest who is unable to sympathize with our weaknesses, but one who in every respect has been tempted as we are, yet without sin. (4:15)

> In the days of his flesh, Jesus offered up prayers and supplications, with loud cries and tears, to him who was able to save him from death, and he was heard because of his reverence. Although he was a son, he learned obedience through what he suffered. (5:7–8)

> Sacrifices and offerings you have not desired, but a body have you prepared for me; in burnt offerings and sin offerings you have taken no pleasure. . . . Behold, I have come to do your will, O God, as it is written of me in the scroll of the book. (10:7)

From all these we can see how, in order to become our Savior, Jesus must face so many troubles. He also must fight against all temptation—from Satan himself, from the Pharisees, from his family, and even from his closest disciples (Matt 16:23).

We tend to underestimate the challenge Jesus faced because we're used to thinking that he is God anyway. Surely Jesus is God, but once he emptied himself he was consistent. He never used his privilege as God to make his mission a bit easier. Therefore, when he saw so many people get hungry after hours of listening to him, he could easily feed five thousand men, not including women and children, with only five loaves and two small fishes.[5] However, when he himself was hungry after forty days of fasting, he refused the temptation of the devil to use his power to transform stone into bread. While on earth, the mighty Savior could feel hungry, thirsty, sad unto death, and amazed, and he could be mocked, hurt, and finally killed at the cross: "he was pierced for our transgressions; he was crushed for our iniquities; upon him was the chastisement that brought us peace, and with his wounds we are healed" (Isa 53:5).

---

5. According to Dr. Stephen Tong, in one of his unpublished sermons, "This miracle is proof that Jesus is God. Because only God can change energy into material. All human being can do is to change material into energy, as we do with the atomic bomb."

Our salvation is not a drama, and Jesus is not a drama king. As the Epistle to the Hebrews says, "Since therefore the children share in flesh and blood, he himself likewise partook of the same things, that through death he might destroy the one who has the power of death, that is, the devil" (2:14). Christ is "to be made like his brothers in every respect" (2:17). He "in every respect has been tempted as we are."

The only thing that makes him different from us is that he never fails; he is "without sin." He never disobeyed, never gave up. On one occasion he said to his disciples, "Now is my soul troubled. And what shall I say? 'Father, save me from this hour'? But for this purpose I have come to this hour. Father, glorify your name" (John 12:28). Jesus refused to pity himself. He persevered until the end and showed reverence to God beyond measure.

We truly cannot overestimate what Christ has done to become a ransom for us. To save us he has to fully pay the debt of our sin to release us from hell, *and* he has to fulfill all requirements of the law to bring us into heaven. We rarely think about these two *distinct* categories seriously and tend to mold them into one. In our mind releasing from hell *means* going to heaven, but in fact they couldn't be more different, just as releasing a prisoner from Alcatraz by no means gives us him right to enter the White House.[6]

Therefore, to bring us into heaven, not only must Christ die in our place, but he must also obey in our place. Christ must walk his life minute by minute in obedience, or there is no heaven for the rest of us. He must obey all the requirements of the law, and he must not fail even once. As Pilate admitted, "I find no guilt in this man" (Luke 23:4). And that is why "being made perfect, he became the source of eternal salvation to all who obey him" (Heb 5:9). Only because Christ has been totally obedient can he present

---

6. Some people believe that in the after life we must suffer for a while to pay for our sins, but after it is done we will be released from hell and be welcomed to heaven. We find two big problems here. First, remembering that we disobey against the *eternal* God, how long do we think our punishment will be? And second, even for the sake of the argument, after we pay it fully, leaving hell is not necessarily the same as entering heaven.

himself as an offering to God, and with that single offering he "has perfected for all time those who are being sanctified" (Heb 10:14).

Thus, through the work of Jesus, as our Savior, we see how great is God's righteousness in saving us eternally. This is the second, and the central, unique quality of the gospel that makes it so irreplaceable. Also from this, we see why Paul understands the gospel as God's power—its first unique quality—because in it God does not merely inform us how to be saved, but he saves us actually. In the redemption fulfilled by the full obedience of Jesus, God has done everything needed to save us. And therefore our salvation is secure. We are truly in a good hands.

Finally, in all this we can see how great is God's love for us, the unworthy. To understand our salvation as an act of a God who is righteous does not diminish our adoration of a God who is love. Love and righteousness belong together.

X

The Two Ways of Salvation

Do you know how many religions exist on this planet? If you answer "so many," then you are almost right. If you say you don't know, then you are perfectly right! In a sense, no one can manage to answer that question, because even the definition of religion itself is debatable.[1] Therefore, the burning question is: how can we claim that the gospel is the only way of salvation when we do not even know about how many religions exist on earth?

The answer for this valid question is that because, while we do not know how to count the religions, we do know there are no more than two ways of salvation on earth since Adam until, at least, the writing of this paragraph. We can only choose—in all possibilities—between salvation *by faith* or salvation *by works*, no more and no less. Furthermore, because of the holiness of God and the pervasiveness of sin in our life, salvation by works is simply not possible. If we want to be saved, we must be saved by faith alone—the third unique quality of the gospel. And finally, because only Christianity manages to offer salvation by faith, then that is why the gospel is the only way of salvation.

---

1. In Indonesia, we once debated about whether we could add to our five official religions a sixth one, Confucianism. Some people objected, for in their opinion we cannot count Confucianism as a religion, because it lacks teaching about God, the afterlife, or supernatural things, and focuses mostly, if not entirely, on ethics and daily life on earth.

Hence, we have arrived at an important summary for our conviction about why the gospel is so irreplaceable: *The salvation that may both satisfy God's righteousness and deal with sin effectively can only be attained by the way of faith, not by the way of works. Since there is no third way of salvation, and since Christianity is the only religion that offers a valid salvation by faith, therefore Christianity is irreplaceable.*

Because we have already said a lot about the nature of God's righteousness and of our sin, we are not going to repeat it again in this chapter. Thus, there are two important questions left for us to explore: (1) why there are only two ways of salvation, which are by faith and by works, and (2) why only Christianity can offer salvation by faith. This chapter will be dealing with the first question, while the second one will be described in the next chapter.

Taking a risk to make this chapter a bit more technical than the rest, I will first of all clear the meaning of these two ways of salvation, starting with the negative one. What I do *not* mean with salvation by works is that it gives no room whatsoever to God or to other supernatural beings. In fact, a religion or a belief may give as much room as possible to God or to other supernatural beings and *still* remain a works religion.

On the other hand, salvation by faith does *not* mean that humankind is only a puppet moved by the higher being or a robot programmed by its creator. Salvation by faith comes about *without* sacrificing even a bit of our nature as human beings. Salvation by faith excludes any boast on the part of us, but it fully includes our mind, emotion, and will.

As the religion offering salvation by faith, Christianity gives as much room as possible for genuine human response. And one of the clearest pieces of evidence for this is the fact that Christianity truly endorses understanding. I would not write this book if I did not believe that. In the Bible we find not only *what* but also *why;* not only statement but also explanation.

That God is willing to explain his grand scheme of salvation to his creatures should make us feel honored. We cannot forget how difficult it was when our kids started using their fingers to point to things around them while asking, "Mom, what is this?" or "Dad, what does that mean?" It is still fresh in my mind, how hard it was to find an answer that is not only right but also can be understood by their very limited capacity. Often I could not help but become irritated and then stopped them from asking more questions. It is just not easy to explain something complex to anyone so simple.

Therefore, it is a great privilege that God is willing to explain to us his secret, which the Bible says "no eye has seen, nor ear heard, nor the heart of man imagined . . ." (1 Cor 2:9). How could flesh and blood like us understand such wisdom of God? One preacher used to say that our fallen mind is "created, limited, and polluted."[2] But still, God chose to reveal *and explain* his divine plan and purpose to us.[3]

Thus, salvation by faith is by no means salvation by blind faith, nor does it mean that we are left with nothing to do. We still have to listen to the gospel, to repent, to confess our sins, to accept Christ as our Lord and Savior, and to walk in the newness of our life. Therefore, as salvation by works does not have to exclude faith in God or other higher beings, neither does salvation by faith exclude human responsibilities. Both look so similar then. Thus, what makes them different?

The difference is that according to salvation by works my eternity will depend *ultimately* on my strength. Yes, someone else, or even God, may help me, show me the way, guide me along that way, and rebuke me when I wander away, but still, the final result will depend on me fulfilling all these requirements. If in the end I happened to fail, then there is nothing God can do to save the day. And there is no guarantee that, at the end of the day, I will be able to fulfill all these requirements and get my proper reward. In other

2. I often heard this statement from Dr. Stephen Tong.

3. Piper (*Brothers*, 97) says, "The implication are huge that God has made a book so crucial in the preservation and declaration of saving truth. These implications become more remarkable because the book has some parts that are really difficult to understand." He urges pastors not to deter to preach from a difficult text. Indeed, a difficult text is a blessing, not a curse.

words, my salvation depends basically and ultimately on myself; it depends on my *work*.

On the other hand, salvation based on faith says,

> Do not say in your heart, "Who will ascend into heaven?" (that is, to bring Christ down) or "Who will descend into the abyss?" (that is, to bring Christ up from the dead). But what does it say? "The word is near you, in your mouth and in your heart" (that is, the word of faith that we proclaim); because, if you confess with your mouth that Jesus is Lord and believe in your heart that God raised him from the dead, you will be saved." . . . *"Everyone who believes in him will not be put to shame"* (Rom 10:8–11, emphasis added).

In salvation by faith, my eternity basically and ultimately depends not on me, but on my Savior. Yes, I still have to repent, to confess, and to bring fruit after I have been saved, but my eternal destiny does not rest on me but on he who has done everything needed for my salvation. In Christian terms, salvation by faith is a "decision to depend on Jesus to save me personally."[4] Or, according to a theologian, faith is "yielding to Christ and trusting in Him for the salvation of the soul."[5] Faith itself "cannot be a meritorious work; it is the response which receives what has already been done for us in Christ."[6] And exactly because of this Paul declares, "For by grace you have been saved through faith. And this is not your own doing; it is the gift of God, not a result of works, so that no one may boast" (Eph 2:8–9).

Notice that I keep using "basically" and "ultimately" here, and that is for a purpose: to show that these two categories are mutually exclusive. The difference between the two ways of salvation is not a matter of degree—which party contributes how much—but about who holds the *final* and *decisive* factor. And for that reason there exists only two possibilities: me *or* not me. These categories are comprehensive—me *or* other but me; they exclude each other.

4. Grudem, *Systematic*, 709–10.

5. Berkhof, *Systematic*, 494.

6. O'Brien, *Ephesians*, 174.

Consequently, we have an *either/or* condition here; *both/and* is simply not possible: whether I *ultimately* depend on my strength to have a better life after death (which is salvation by works) or whether I *totally* surrender my eternal destiny to God (and am saved by faith alone).

Thus, there are only two ways of salvation on earth: by faith or by works. And only the first one works. One day, a member of my congregation told me about her mother's conversion to Jesus. Her mother was a very devout woman of another religion who thought that it is absurd that people can be saved just because someone else wants to die for them. For her, to be saved one must keep doing the right things and not just believe in a Savior.

Not wanting to debating her own mother, she merely asked her mother to count how many days in her life she is able to not sin. It was a surprise to her that one day her mother came and told her that she wants to believe in Jesus. Her mother confessed that after two years trying she had given up; not even one single day had she succeeded! She finally admitted that the Savior is a must.

Indeed, the savior is a must. Because we can only be saved by faith alone.

XI

The Only Salvation by Faith

IN CHAPTER FOUR WE read about my conversation with a good Muslim who believed that he was saved by *rahmat Allah,* their term for what we call "God's grace." When I asked him about how a righteous God could pour out his grace on sinners instead of punishing them properly, he admitted that in his faith this is *ga'ib,* which means something so deep it cannot be comprehended or explained. This conversation underlines that while there are two ways of salvation, only Christianity offers salvation by faith. The other religions have no choice but to embrace salvation by works. This good Muslim thought he was saved by *rahmat Allah,* but at the same time he had to admit that this *rahmat,* as wonderful as it is, has no solid ground.

Some have difficulty accepting salvation by faith because, for them, it is way too easy. After so many years committing so many sins and transgressions, how could it be that all we have to do is believe and then everything will be fine? For them, this way of salvation is simply too good to be true. But this is only a half truth, for faith itself is not groundless. The fact that only Christianity offers this kind of salvation is telling evidence that salvation by faith is not as simple as what people think. If salvation by faith is indeed way too easy, surely many or even all religions have a chance to offer the same thing if they want to, do they not?

But faith is not a subjective thing inside me that is able to create a reality from what I believe. Faith itself creates nothing;

what matters most is not the faith itself but the object of faith. We are saved by faith, but it is not our faith itself that saves us; our salvation depends on what we put our faith in.

As a comparison, if I'm ill, in order to be healed I need faith. If I refuse to believe in any doctor, then I will not go to any of them and cannot be healed, even if some of them might have the right medication. On the other hand, no matter how much I believe in a doctor to heal my sickness, the fact is that if he gives me a wrong medication then my disease will not heal and I will still be ill. Indeed, even if I trust him and obey his prescription down to the minutest detail, if his diagnose is false and his medication misses the mark, then I am not going to heal.

As another example, when I take my son to have dinner in a restaurant, he trusts me to pay the bill. He will not keep asking about how much we have spent for our meal. He has no worry about that. He only need to focus on finishing the meal he has already ordered. But if I somehow forget to bring my wallet, then his faith means nothing. If I cannot handle the situation, then he will get into trouble, no matter how big is his faith on me.

Back to our discussion, we may believe that we are saved by faith. But the most decisive question is in whom we put our faith. When this question is asked of Christians, we may answer that we are saved by faith in Jesus Christ, who has died as our redemption. We are saved by faith because we put our faith in he "who was delivered up for our trespasses and raised for our justification" (Rom 4:25). We put our faith fully in Jesus, for we know who he is, what he has done, and why he is able to save wretches like us. This is the core of salvation by faith.

This is also the very reason why only Christianity may offer salvation by faith: because only Christianity has a savior who is fully qualified to redeem his people. Without a qualified savior, we are left to save our own life by our own strength. For without a savior, in whom will we put our faith? Who has to pay the bill of our transgression? We may say that we trust in God to save us, but what would that supposedly mean? What has God done to save us? How has he provided a way of salvation that is fully valid? For the alternative is that we believe that he will save us in a groundless way, or for a *ga'ib* reason.

Thus, it is great that we believe God will save us, but how? In what way will God save us? Will he give us direction, command, illumination, guidance, etc., and then leave us to determine our own salvation by trying to follow his direction, command, or guidance? Or will he fulfill by himself every term and condition of our salvation, and then save those who humbly come to him to be saved? As we have discussed, the first option is salvation by works; the second one is by faith. Only Christianity can be the second one because only Christianity believes in a God who in Jesus Christ already did whatever it takes to save those who believe in him.

So finally we comeback to our summary: *The salvation that may both satisfy God's righteousness and deal with sin effectively can only be attained by the way of faith, not by the way of works. Since there is no third way of salvation and since Christianity is the only religion that offers a valid salvation by faith, therefore Christianity is irreplaceable.*

Many people have difficulty seeing the Christian faith as irreplaceable, for in their understanding there are so many religions on this planet, all with their own uniqueness, and it is by no means easy to compare one with others. Therefore, how can one single religion claim itself as the only true religion? But if what I argued above is sustainable—if there are only *two* ways of salvation, *either* by works *or* by faith; *either* it *ultimately* depends on me *or* not on me—then things will become much clearer.

If I can be saved by my good deeds, then the claim that Christianity is irreplaceable is simply false. If there is any possibility to be saved by works, then Christianity may offer a workable way of salvation, but so do others. However, if there is no possibility to be saved by works and if there is a sure salvation by faith, then we can rightly claim that Christianity is irreplaceable because only Christianity offers salvation that is by faith alone.

XII

How Can We Be So Sure?

WHAT IF, AS WE are lying in our deathbed and gathering our children and our family around us, one among them comes close to us and says, "Please do not be afraid! We promise that we will continually pray so that you can be accepted by our God"?

I can guarantee you, a dying Buddhist or Muslim parent will truly rejoice in his or her heart hearing this. As an Indonesian with Chinese background, I learned that Chinese people, mostly followers of Buddhism or Confucianism, value prayers for deceased parents as extremely high in importance. Similarly, in conversations with Muslims I find that they generally believe that their salvation, to a certain extent, depends on the prayers of their descendants.

But not if we are Christians! Without exaggeration, I dare say that, among all who believe in the afterlife, Christians are the only ones who will be troubled by their children's eagerness to pray for their salvation after they are deceased. An atheist would probably just ignore such nonsense, nor would an agnostic care, but only a true Christian will be disturbed by this. We would be so disturbed by the fact that our own beloved children still have no certainty about the final destination of their parent in Christ. Yes, one distinct characteristic of Christians is the firm conviction of their salvation. This assurance often perplexes many people. They usually ask, "These people have not yet been in heaven, have they? Do they think they are good enough to inherit heaven? How can they be so sure?"

A Christian woman once confronted me about my Reformed faith, that once a Christian is truly saved, forever he or she is saved. She said that she cannot agree with that doctrine. As a response I asked her a personal question: "With all respect, in case you must leave this world tomorrow, are you sure that God will accept you?" I still remember she firmly declared, "Yes, I am sure he will receive me." In my humble experience, I have found that *both* Calvinist *and* Armenian sides feel such an assurance in their hearts. Somehow they are convinced that they are the sons and daughters of the living God, that he will accept them with arms wide open once they are coming home, and they have no worry that the angel of the Lord will not allow them to enter the heavenly gate.

Luther did not miss the mark when he said, "We must by all means believe for a certainty . . . that we are pleasing to God for the sake of Christ."[1] And we also concur with Calvin, who, although realizing that "we cannot imagine any certainty that is not tinged with doubt, or any assurance that is not assailed by some anxiety," denied that "in whatever way they are afflicted, believers [can] fall away and depart from the certain assurance received from God's mercy."[2] These two giants of the Reformation confirmed that such a blessed assurance is a normal experience for Christians.

But still, this kind of assurance is *not* ordinary. We will hardly find this kind of conviction in our life. First of all, no other religion provides such a firm warranty. Muslims love to say "*Insya Allah*," which more or less means "*if* God is willing." As good as the meaning of this blessing is, *if* is different than *sure*. Similarly, Chinese culture has erudite mourning rituals for the deceased because, in their contention, the journey of those who have already passed away is not over yet: we must assist them from earth, and *hopefully* things turn out to be good for them.

Therefore, Christianity is very unique. We even call our mourning ritual a consolation because our focus is *not* to pray for the dying, but to comfort the living. Buddhist parents find it hard to understand why their children refuse to pray for their ancestors

1. Luther, *Lectures on Galatians*, 377.
2. Calvin, *Institutes*, book 3, ch. 2.17.

once they become Christians. This is not because Christians do not respect their ancestors, but because we believe that one's destiny is fixed with one's last breath. There is nothing we can do to change that even a little bit. And this kind of belief is truly rare.

Secondly, this kind of certainty is not "normal" because, while we may feel certain about some routines and ordinary things, we hardly have such confidence about the extraordinary ones. We have no doubt that the sun will shine tomorrow, for example. But the existence of heaven and hell is a whole different story. We never see its advertising. We never taste it directly. Although we may have heard that some have visited there, but whether this testimony is true or false, it has a small, if any, effect on our certainty. Therefore, while on the one hand it is normal for Christians to have such an assurance, on the other hand the question lingers: how can we be as sure about heaven as we are about the sun?

According to the Bible, our assurance is not caused by psychological or sociological factors, but by a spiritual power: "The Spirit himself bears witness with our spirit that we are children of God" (Rom 8:16). This testimony from the deepest point of our being is the source of our full assurance.

Thirdly, we can be so sure because our salvation is indeed truly solid. And our salvation is that solid because the way Christ redeemed us is righteous from start to finish. All Torah has been fulfilled in Christ! Therefore, the ultimate Judge can, in full justice, declares in his courtroom that we are free instead of guilty. And because God's courtroom is the highest one, no one can appeal to another courtroom and no other courtroom may cancel the verdict. When the Judge of all nations has declared that we are justified in Christ, and when this declaration is built on the solid, righteous work of Christ, this decree is unbreakable. And that is why the Spirit can work such a firm assurance in our heart.

Even the Accuser himself must admit it, whether he likes it or not. In Romans 8:32 Paul can declare the challenge, "Who shall bring any *charge* against God's elect?" (emphasis added). In the Bible, the word "charge" has a special connection with the work of the devil himself, who builds his reputation as the Great Accuser, as we can see in the story of Job. In accusing Job, Satan showed his shrewdness: he managed to accuse even a man as blameless and upright as Job (Job 1:9). And even after his first accusation had failed, he did not give up easily and still managed to get one more chance (2:4–5).

Reflection on this brought my memory to a film entitled *Intolerable Cruelty*, starred by George Clooney and Catherine Zeta-Jones. In the opening scene, a husband who is found cheating by his wife comes to a lawyer because she has asked for divorce. He refused to share anything with her, although his cheating had been videotaped. When the client asked, "Is that possible?" the lawyer replied, "It's a challenge." To make the story short, this lawyer finally succeed overcoming this challenge: his client's wife had to go with nothing! I dare not judge that all great lawyers will be similar to this one. But even if they are, the Accuser will overcome all of them. He is the Great Prosecutor. He always manages to find a crack, no matter how small it is, and he squeezes it to his advantage.

Job is hardly his only victim. And he always targets a high and noble object. In Zechariah 3:1 we read, "Then he showed me Joshua the high priest standing before the angel of the LORD, and Satan standing at his right hand to accuse him." Even our Lord himself did not escape, although he won a definitive victory. But even after his miserable failure the devil "departed from him *until an opportune time*" (Luke 4:13, emphasis added). If there is anything we can learn from our enemy, it is his great zeal and his perseverance.

Putting Romans 8:32 into this context, we wonder: how can Paul be so sure in declaring that our salvation is accusation-free? How dare he challenge even Satan himself? The answer is of course not because Paul has huge self-confidence, but because he knows God's way of salvation is so righteous that it leaves not even the smallest fissure. Indeed, our salvation is undisputable not because we are transformed into angels once we believe in Jesus; we are still sinning, and some even sinning grievously. What Luther said is so true: all Christians are "*simul iustus et peccator*," which means "at the same time righteous and a sinner." If the Accuser has no chance in accusing us, it is not because he cannot find a hole in us, but because—and only because—the blood of our Savior has covered all the holes. As a loud voice in heaven has said,

> Now the salvation and the power and the kingdom of our God and the authority of his Christ have come, for the accuser of our brothers has been thrown down, who accuses them day and night before our God. And they have conquered him by the blood of the Lamb and by the word of their testimony, for they loved not their lives even unto death. (Rev 12:10–12)

While not forgetting the importance of faithfulness in the part of believers, this verse clearly declares that the persistent Accuser can be conquered only by the blood of Jesus. And only his love make us "more than conquerors" (Rom 8:37). Therefore Paul, in another letter, may claim the total victory:

> And you, who were dead in your trespasses and the uncircumcision of your flesh, God made alive together with him, having forgiven us all our trespasses, by canceling the record of debt that stood against us with its legal demands. This he set aside, nailing it to the cross. He disarmed the rulers and authorities and put them to open shame, by triumphing over them in him. (Col 2:14–15)

That is why righteousness matter. Justification built upon mere love is fragile; it cannot stand in the courtroom because only justice will prevail there. Even our archenemy has to admit it. Satan cannot bring any charge because there is not even the slightest crack in God's way of salvation: God is fully righteous in declaring us not guilty; the process is clean from start to finish, from planning to execution to implementation. There is no injustice in God, and there is no injustice in his work of salvation. When the highest court has justified us on the base of faultless procedure, then the full assurance is ours.

With this we come to the end of our discussion. We have already discussed three unique qualities of the gospel: it is powerful (chapter 2), righteous (chapters 3–9), and by faith alone (chapters 10–11). In addition to that, in this chapter we have discussed the assurance of those who believe in Jesus. Our salvation is so sure. Just as the gospel is also so irreplaceable.

Bibliography

Berkhof, Louis. *Systematic Theology.* Grand Rapids: Eerdmans, 1996.

Calvin, John. *Institutes of the Christian Religion.* Edited by John T. McNeill. 2 vols. Library of Christian Classics. Philadelphia: Westminster, 1960.

Grudem, Wayne. *Systematic Theology.* Grand Rapids: Zondervan, 1994.

Hawkins, Greg, and Cally Parkinson. *Move: What 1,000 Churches Reveal about Spiritual Growth.* Grand Rapids: Zondervan, 2011.

Hoekema, Anthony. *Created in God's Image.* Grand Rapids: Eerdmans, 1994.

Jenkins, Phillip. *The Next Christendom: The Coming of Global Christianity.* Rev. ed. New York: Oxford University Press, 2007.

Luther, Martin. *Lectures on Galatians.* Edited by Jaroslav Pelikan. 2 vols. Luther's Works 26, 27. St. Louis: Concordia, 1963, 1964.

Moo, Douglas. *The Epistle to the Romans.* New International Commentary on the New Testament. Grand Rapids: Eerdmans, 1996.

Mouw, Richard. *Uncommon Decency: Christian Civility in an Uncivil World.* Rev. ed. Downers Grove, IL: InterVarsity, 2010.

Neill, Stephen, and Owen Chadwick. *A History of Christian Missions.* 2nd ed. Pelican History of the Church 6. London: Penguin, 1990.

O'Brien, Peter. *The Letter to the Ephesians.* Pillar New Testament Commentary. Grand Rapids: Eerdmans, 1999.

——— . *The Letter to the Hebrews.* Pillar New Testament Commentary. Grand Rapids: Eerdmans, 2010.

Piper, John. *Brothers, We Are Not Professionals: A Plea to Pastors for Radical Ministry.* Nashville: Broadman & Holman, 2002.

Schnabel, Eckhard. *Early Christian Mission.* 2 vols. Downers Grove, IL: InterVarsity, 2004.

Schreiner, Thomas. *Romans.* Baker Exegetical Commentary on the New Testament. Grand Rapids: Baker, 1998.

Yandell, Keith, and Harold Netland, *Buddhism: A Christian Exploration and Appraisal.* Downers Grove, IL: IVP Academic, 2009.

www.ingramcontent.com/pod-product-compliance
Lightning Source LLC
Chambersburg PA
CBHW071109090426
42737CB00013B/2547